SCHOTT'S SPORTING
GAMING & IDLING
MISCELLANY

SCHOTT'S SPORTING GAMING & IDLING MISCELLANY

Conceived, written, and designed by

BEN SCHOTT

BLOOMSBURY

Schott's Sporting, Gaming, & Idling Miscellany™

© BEN SCHOTT 2004

Published by Bloomsbury Publishing Plc
38 Soho Square, London, W1D 3HB, UK

www.miscellanies.info

10 9 8 7 6 5 4 3 2 1

Also by Ben Schott and published by Bloomsbury
Schott's Original Miscellany and *Schott's Food & Drink Miscellany*

ISBN 0-7475-6924-X
A CIP catalogue record for this book is available from the British Library.

Under the terms of the 1961 Printer's Imprint Act, a legal obligation exists to include,
on the first or last leaf, the name and usual place of business of the printer of all books
published in the UK. Curiously, except in the case of election literature, there is no
such obligation to print the name of the publisher – perhaps because the original
legislation dates to a time when printer and publisher tended to be one and the same.

Designed and typeset by BEN SCHOTT
Printed in Great Britain by CLAYS Ltd., ST IVES Plc.

SCHOTT'S SPORTING GAMING & IDLING MISCELLANY

A score-card? A rule-book? A handicap certificate? A team-sheet?
A betting-slip? A dance-card? A note from matron?

Schott's Sporting, Gaming, & Idling Miscellany is the third snapper-up of unconsidered trifles. Its purpose is to keep wicket at the conversational crease. In doing so, the *Miscellany* casts its net wide across the sporting field, gathering in everything from the Noble Art and the Beautiful Game, to the Sport of Kings and the Gentle Craft (see p.140).

But all this frenetic activity is bound to be tiring, certainly for the more sedate gamesters and speculators amongst us. So, alongside field sports, team sports, winter sports, and Olympic sports the armchair athlete will find board games, parlour games, drinking games, and gambling.

And, in pursuit of the complete spectrum of human (in)activity (see p.152), *Schott's Sporting, Gaming, & Idling Miscellany* turns its attention to the ultimate pastimes of indolence, from cards, crosswords, and shadow patterns to bathing, sleeping, and dreaming. Essential reading for idlers, loafers, and *flâneurs* – if they can summon up the energy.

––––––––––––––––– VERY DULL –––––––––––––––––

Painstaking efforts have been made to ensure that all of the information contained within the *Miscellany* is correct. However, as Oliver Goldsmith noted, 'a book may be amusing with numerous errors, or it may be very dull without a single absurdity'. The author can accept no responsibility if you get your conker stamped on; catch a chill streaking; shoot a beater; unnecessarily pull in at the pits; raise a royal flush; *fizz* when you should have *buzzed*; or maim yourself horribly somewhere down the Cresta Run.

If you have any suggestions[†], corrections, clarifications, or stretching exercises, please email them to idling@miscellanies.info – or send them c/o Bloomsbury Publishing Plc., 38 Soho Square, London, W1D 3HB, UK.

† The author reserves the right to treat suggestions and exercises as his own, and to use them in future editions, other projects, or to help lend him a lithe and svelte appearance.

The following have been selected for the squad:

Jonathan[s], Judith[g], and Geoffrey[i] Schott.

Richard Album[s], Clare Algar[i], Juliet Aston[i],
Stephen Aucutt[g], Joanna Begent[g], Martin Birchall[g],
John Casey[i], Andrew Cock[s], James Coleman[g],
Martin Colyer[i], Victoria Cook[i], Aster Crawshaw[i],
Rosemary Davidson[i], Jody Davies[s], Liz Davies[s],
Ellie Dorday[i], Will Douglas[g], Jennifer Epworth[i],
Kathleen Farrar[i], Minna Fry[g], Penny Gillinson[i],
Gaynor Hall[g], Charlotte Hawes[g], Max Jones[s],
Robert Klaber[s], Hugo de Klee[g], Lisa Koenigsberg[g],
Alison Lang[g], Rachel Law[i], John Lloyd[s], David Loewi[i],
Ruth Logan[i], Chris Lyon[i], Jess Manson[s],
Michael Manson[s], Sarah Marcus[i], Susannah McFarlane[i],
Peter McIntyre[i], Colin Midson[g], David Miller[i],
Polly Napper[i], Sarah Norton[g], Mark Owen[s],
Cally Poplak[i], Dave Powell[s], Alexandra Pringle[i],
Daniel Rosenthal[s], Tom Rosenthal[s], Sarah Sands[s],
Ian Scaramanga[s], Carolyne Sibley[g], Rachel Simhon[i],
James Spackman[s], Amy Stanton[s], Claire Starkey[g],
Bill Swainson[s], Matthew Thornley[g], David Ward[i],
Ann Warnford-Davis[i], William Webb[s], and Caitlin Withey[i].

The full team will be posted up on the board on the day of the match.
Could everyone please ensure that *this* time they have the right kit.

Key to preferred activity: [s]porting · [g]aming · [i]dling

Sincere thanks are extended to Graeme Garden and 'Dickie' Bird.

Serious SPORT has nothing to do with fair play
… it is war minus the shooting.

— GEORGE ORWELL (1903–50)

Man is a GAMING animal. He must always be
trying to get the better in something or other.

— CHARLES LAMB (1775–1834)

It is impossible to enjoy IDLING thoroughly
unless one has plenty of work to do.

— JEROME K. JEROME (1859–1927)

―――――――――― CRICKETING DUCKS ――――――――――

DUCK† .... given out without having scored a single run
A PAIR (OF SPECTACLES) .... ducks in both innings of a match
GOLDEN DUCK .... given out on one's first ball
A KING PAIR .... golden ducks in both innings of a match
SILVER DUCK .... given out on the second ball of match (?)
DIAMOND DUCK .... given out on the first ball of a match (?)
PLATINUM DUCK .... given out on the first ball of a season (?)

† The term *duck* derives from the shape of the number zero, which resembles a duck's egg.
The Primary Club is a cricketing charity founded in 1955 to support sporting and
recreational facilities for the visually impaired. Membership of the club is open to all, but
especially welcome are those who have been given out first-ball at any level of the game.
(Entries marked with a question mark are at best tentative and at worst utterly spurious.)
Of course, in the game of French Cricket (see p.53) one cannot be out on the first ball.

―――――――――― DEATH & LAUGHTER ――――――――――

CHALCHAS · A soothsayer who died laughing at the thought that he had outlived the time he predicted for his own death.

ZEUXIS · The C5thBC painter who died laughing at the sight of an old hag whom he had just painted.

PHILOMENES · Died laughing at the sight of an ass eating his figs.

MARGUTTE · A giant who died of laughter watching a monkey trying to put on a pair of boots.

TOMMY COOPER · True giant of comedy who died on stage to the sound of laughter, 15 April 1984.

CRASSUS · Died from laughing on seeing an ass eat thistles.

MRS FITZHERBERT · Died on 19 April 1782 at the Drury Lane Theatre while laughing at the poor performance of an actor.

For details of the Burmese king who died laughing, see p.50 of *Schott's Original Miscellany.*

―――――――――― A REMEDY FOR IDLENESS ――――――――――

It has been advised for a fit of idleness, to sit down and count the ticking of a clock for one hour, and the individual will be thankful to get up and work like a native, rather than spend another hour in the same manner.

— ANONYMOUS, *Advice to the million by a friend to the people*, or *How to live and enjoy sound vigorous health on sixpence per day*, *c.*1830

WONDERLAND CROQUET

'Get to your places!' shouted the Queen in a voice of thunder, and people began running about in all directions, tumbling up against each other; however, they got settled down in a minute or two, and the game began. Alice thought she had never seen such a curious croquet-ground in her life; it was all ridges and furrows; the balls were live hedgehogs, the mallets live flamingoes, and the soldiers had to double themselves up and to stand on their hands and feet, to make the arches. The chief difficulty Alice found at first was in managing her flamingo: she succeeded in getting its body tucked away, comfortably enough, under her arm, with its legs hanging down, but generally, just as she had got its neck nicely straightened out, and was going to give the hedgehog a blow with its head,

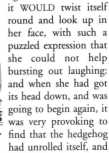

it WOULD twist itself round and look up in her face, with such a puzzled expression that she could not help bursting out laughing: and when she had got its head down, and was going to begin again, it was very provoking to find that the hedgehog had unrolled itself, and was in the act of crawling away: besides all this, there was generally a ridge or furrow in the way wherever she wanted to send the hedgehog to, and, as the doubled-up soldiers were always getting up and walking off to other parts of the ground, Alice soon came to the conclusion that it was a very difficult game indeed.

— LEWIS CARROLL, *Alice's Adventures in Wonderland*, 1865
[illustration by Sir John Tenniel]

SNOOKER BALL VALUES

Red	1	Brown	4	Black	7
Yellow	2	Blue	5	Orange[†]	8
Green	3	Pink	6	Purple[†]	10

† These two balls were introduced into a variant of the standard game called Snooker Plus – devised by the world snooker and billiard champion Joe Davis in response to fears that the popularity of snooker was in decline. Davis proposed that a purple ball be placed between brown and blue, and an orange ball between blue and pink, in the hope that this would encourage break building. The addition of these two colours meant that the maximum possible break increased from 147[‡] to 210. Snooker Plus was introduced to the public in October 1959 during a *News of the World* tournament, but never really took off.
‡ It is possible to have a break of 155 assuming that it starts with a free-ball red and black.

─────── THE LANGUAGE OF FALCONRY ───────

Falconry is the art of training and employing birds of prey – falcons or hawks – in the service of man. It seems that China knew falconry as far back as 2000BC (the Chinese even hunted butterflies with hawks), and Japan knew the sport around 600BC. From these civilisations, and the trade routes they developed, falconry travelled West, where it was embraced by the Mongols, Persians, and Arabs before sweeping across Europe. Although under English law (e.g. the Forest Charter of 1217) any free man could own a hawk, from its arrival in Britain falconry was considered a noble, aristocratic, and essentially regal activity. (This was in part guaranteed by the cost of the birds, the elaborate diet they were fed, and the extensive training they required.) Falcons were exchanged as gifts by monarchs, and were even considered to be appropriate exchanges for aristocratic prisoners of war. Kings in succession framed legislation to protect their rights to keep and hunt with hawks – under Edward III the stealing of a hawk became punishable by death. The class distinction of falconry embraced not only which type of hawk might be owned by which rank of individual (see p.118), but also the complex vocabulary which hawksmen employed. As Ben Jonson wrote, 'to speak the hawking language was affected by the 'newer man' who aped the manners of the older gentry'. Some of falconry's poetic terms are translated below:

Hawks do not breed but *eyer*, and are not hatched but *disclosed*. Hawks are *reclaimed* not tamed, and they are not trained but *made* or *manned*. Hawks do not chase animals, they *fly after fur*, *after feather*, or *after plume* and, when they have sighted their prey, hawks do not swoop but *stoop* to attack the *inke* (neck) of their quarry. Once killed that quarry becomes a *pelt*, not to digest but to *endew* especially if the hawk is hungry or *sharp set*. After a meal hawks do not preen themselves but *rejoice*, and they do not clean their beaks, rather they *freak* them. Such a distinguished creature would never moult, instead they *mew*†. Hawks do not perch but *take stand*; they do not drink but *bowse*; they do not sleep but *jenk*; they *bate* rather than beat their wings; and do not shake their feathers, rather they *rouse* them. They do not fight with other birds, rather they *crab*. A hawk is never fat or overweight, but *high* and, when high, will be *enseamed* to purge excess weight. A hawk is never constipated, but suffers from *craye*, and does not cough but *keck*. Of course, hawks are never actually ill – rather they are said to suffer from *ungladness*.

† We derive 'mews' from the buildings where hawks were kept while they moulted (or mewd) – mew comes from the Latin *mutare*, 'to change'. Our current use of mews to describe where horses are stabled dates back to 1534 when the Royal Mews in Charing Cross, London, (originally the home of the King's hawks) were given over to horses.

———————— THE WACKY RACES ————————

In Hanna-Barbera's cartoon series *The Wacky Races*, 11 teams competed for the title of the 'World's Wackiest Racer' – no doubt inspired by Blake Edwards' 1966 film *The Great Race*. The wacky vehicles and drivers were:

No.	Vehicle	Drivers
00	The Mean Machine	Dick Dastardly, and Muttley
01	The Bouldermobile	The Slag Brothers: Rock & Gravel
02	The Creepy Coupe	The Gruesome Twosome
03	The Ring-a-Ding Convert-a-Car	Professor Pat Pending
04	The Crimson Haybailer	The Red Max
05	The Compact Pussycat	Penelope Pitstop
06	The Army Surplus Special	The Sarge, and Private Meekly
07	The Bullet Proof Bomb	The Ant Hill Mob†
08	The Arkansas Chug-a-Bug	Luke & Blubber Bear
09	The Turbo Terrific	Peter Perfect
10	The Buzzwagon	Rufus Ruffcut, and Sawtooth

† The Ant Hill Mob (voiced entirely by Mel Blanc) was comprised of Clyde, Zippy, Softy, Ding-a-Ling, Pockets, Snoozy, and Yak-Yak. A somewhat reconfigured Ant Hill Mob appeared in a spin-off cartoon series, *The Perils of Penelope Pitstop*, driving Chugga-Boom.

———————— THE JOY OF BACKGAMMON ————————

Backgammon has always been a fire-side, a domestic, a conjugal game; it is not so abstruse as to banish conversation on general topics; it does not like chess, or love, or art, or science, require the entire man, whilst the ever-recurring rattle of the dice keeps the ear alert and the attention alive; it has often been found an anodyne to the gout, the rheumatism, the azure devils, or the 'yellow spleen'.

— GEORGE FREDERICK PARDON, *Backgammon*, 1844

———————— ON WOMEN PLAYING TENNIS ————————

WILFRED BADDELEY · 1895
'If a lady intends to play lawn tennis, the first thing she must make up her mind to do is run about, and not merely take those balls that come straight to her, giving up the others as too difficult.'

RICHARD KRAJICEK · 1992
'80% of the women playing at Wimbledon are lazy, fat pigs and shouldn't be allowed on the show courts.' (The next day Krajicek clarified his position: 'I said 80% of the top 100 are fat pigs but I just over-exaggerated a little bit. What I meant was only 75%.')

———— 'P COMPANY' SELECTION TESTS ————

The British army's Pre-Parachute Selection test is the antithesis of idling. The tough mission statement of P Company, as it is known, is as follows:

> *To test physical fitness, determination and mental robustness, under conditions of stress, to determine whether an individual has the self discipline and motivation required for service with Airborne Forces.*

P Company has a three-week build-up before a final week of eight tests:

10 MILE MARCH · Carrying a 35lb pack and individual weapon. To be completed in 1 hour 50 mins.

TRAINASIUM · A pass/fail aerial confidence course – the highest point of which is 60ft.

LOG RACE · An 8-man team race carrying a log weighing *c.*175kg around a 1.8 mile course.

2 MILE RUN · Carrying a 35lb pack and individual weapon. To be completed in 18 minutes.

STEEPLECHASE · A 1·7 mile course with 25 obstacles. To be completed in under 19 minutes.

MILLING · A 1 minute bout of sparring† with 16oz boxing gloves. Soldiers stand squarely in the centre of a ring and throw as many punches as possible at the head and torso of their opponent within the time limit. 'Boxing' and self-defence are not allowed.

20 MILE ENDURANCE MARCH · Carrying 35lb pack and individual weapon. To be completed in 4 hours 50 minutes.

STRETCHER RACE · A team event with up to 18 men per team, carrying stretcher over a 5 mile course. Only 4 men are allowed to carry the stretcher at any one time.

† Milling aims to test 'controlled aggression' against an opponent of similar height, age and weight – it is scored from 0–10: 'Failing to display any qualities of an Airborne Soldier' scores 0; 'Showed more interest in protecting himself than fighting. Limited will to win and aggression' scores 4; and 'Displayed very high levels of courage, determination and fitness. Despite relentless punishment he kept his head up and fought' scores 10.

———————— CRAPS ————————

Craps is a dice game devised in the C19th by Bernard de Mandeville which he developed from the game of hazard. With two dice, players lose on their first roll if they throw 2, 3, or 12 (craps), but win with 7 or 11. If the player's first throw is 4, 5, 6, 8, 9, or 10, this number becomes the *point*, and the player continues until they throw the *point* again (*makes the point*), thereby winning, or until they throw a 7, thereby losing (*craps out*).

SCORING JOUSTS

Originally a training exercise for war, jousting (or tilting) developed into part of the entertainment at C12th tournaments. (Although jousting to the death – *à outrance* – remained an accepted method of duelling.) Two mounted knights rode on either side of a wooden divide (the tilt), aiming their heavy lances at the head or shield of their opponent with the goal of unseating them. Generally each knight rode between 3 and 6 courses, and their scores were marked by heralds on 'jousting cheques'. Four things were marked with ink or by pin-prick on the lines of these cheques: hits on the opposition; lances broken; lances disallowed; and courses run:

The scoring system itself was not only highly convoluted but it seems to have varied from region to region and over the years. For example, breaking a spear while unhorsing an opponent usually scored +3 points, but striking the tilt by mistake cost -2 points. Striking a horse, an opponent in the back, or an opponent after they had been disarmed, or striking the tilt three times all led to the disqualification of the knight.

THE MARATHON

In 490BC, the Greek soldier Pheidippides[†] ran from Marathon to Athens, a distance said to be around 23 miles, to break to the Athenians the news that the Persians had been defeated in battle. After imparting his message, Pheidippides dropped stone dead. At the first modern Olympic Games in Athens (1896), a race was held of approximately the same length to commemorate Pheidippides' run, and the marathon was born. At the first few Olympics the marathon was run over 26 miles. At the 'suggestion' of Queen Alexandra (consort to Edward VII) the marathon at the 1908 London Olympics was extended by 385 yards so that it started on the lawn of Windsor Castle on its way to the Olympic stadium in White City. This allowed Princess Mary and her children to watch the start from the nursery window. To this day some of the more sarcastic marathon runners shout 'God Save the Queen' as they pass the 26-mile mark. In 1924 this arbitrary distance became the standard length of a marathon.

[†] There is some debate as to whether it was actually Pheidippides who made this famous journey. It seems likely that it was Pheidippides who ran the 150 miles from Athens to Sparta to enlist support *before* the battle. However, opinion is divided as to whether he or an unknown courier made the fatal run back from Marathon.

BUMBLEPUPPY

The term Bumblepuppy has been ascribed to a variety of games: a form of racket-ball where the aim is to wrap a ball around a post to which it is attached with string (later popularised as swingball); a version of *al fresco* bagatelle played with lead balls; and most commonly, perhaps, any casual or unrefined game of bridge or whist. W. Somerset Maughan once wrote:

> Templeton isn't the sort of chap to play bumble-puppy bridge
> with a girl like that unless he's getting something out of it.

YABBA

Stephen Harold 'Yabba' Gascoine (1878–1942) was a Balmain rabbit hawker ('rabbito') who gained fame as Australia's most celebrated cricket barracker. Nicknamed Yabba either because he talked too much, or because it was a corruption or his hawking-cry 'rabbo', Gascoine's verbal assaults were legendary on the Hill at Sydney Cricket Ground. A selection of his taunts, many of which have entered cricket's vernacular, include:

> Your length's lousy, but you bowl a good width!
> You'll have to call the fire brigade to get him out!
> Don't worry, mate – with that ball he would have bowled me!
> Send 'im down a piano, see if 'e can play that!
> Gee, I wish you were a statue and I were a pigeon!

The legendary Jack Hobbs made a point of meeting Yabba after playing his final test at Sydney in 1929, and when Yabba died the spectators on the Hill stood in silence as a (perhaps ironic) mark of respect. An obituary of the gravel-voiced barracker stated: 'Just as there can be only one Victor Trumper and one Don Bradman, there can be only one Yabba' – a claim justified by his inclusion in Australia's *Dictionary of National Biography.*

THE 7 DEADLY SINS OF GOLF

Apart from *Missing the Globe* (failing to hit the ball at all) golf's 7 sins are:

Topping..........striking the top of the ball with the bottom of the club
Duffing ....hitting the ground before the ball
Sclaffing ....skidding the club over the grass before it hits the ball
Heeling and *Toeing* .....hitting the ball with either of the edges of a club
Slicing....................when the ball is sliced to the right by the club
Pulling...................when the ball to the left is hooked by the club

THE POOH STICKS BRIDGE

The game of Pooh Sticks was introduced to the world in A.A. Milne's timeless classic *Winnie the Pooh* (1926). The game involves dropping a number of sticks over one side of a bridge and seeing which emerges first on the other. It is generally considered to be a Very Relaxing Game. The bridge upon which Milne and his son Christopher stood and played Pooh Sticks is located in Ashdown Forest in East Sussex; it was built in 1907 by John C. Osman, and was originally known as Posingford Bridge. The architectural diagram below shows both plan and elevation of the Pooh Sticks Bridge, as well as suggesting an ideal 'Racing Line' for Pooh Sticks:

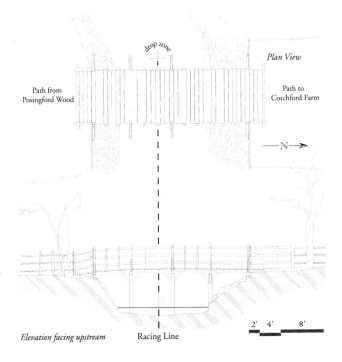

drop zone

Plan View

Path from
Posingford Wood

Path to
Cotchford Farm

→ N →

2' 4' 8'

Elevation facing upstream Racing Line

Field research indicates that adopting the Racing Line illustrated above can reduce a stick's time by up to 5 seconds. Clearly, the Racing Line will be influenced by a range of seasonal conditions including weather, water flow, and atmospheric pressure, as well as assorted flotsam and jetsam.

——— ON THE CLASSIFICATION OF DOODLES ———

Doodles are sketches or scribbles drawn while the attention of the conscious mind is elsewhere. Sadly, little research appears to have been undertaken into this fascinating field of human idleness. However, in 1938 Dr W.S. Maclay et al. [*Proc Roy Soc Med* 1938; 31:1337–50] undertook an analysis of 9,000 doodles that had been sent in to a newspaper by its readers. (The paper promised to have the doodles analysed by an 'expert psychologist', and to award prizes.) Maclay classified the doodles thus:

type	composition	%
Scenes	*resembling an ordinary representation of a subject*	11
Medley	*stray, well spaced, items, independent of each other*	38
Mixture	*independent items, overlapping or intermingling*	32
Scribbles	*unelaborate lines or scrawls*	7
Ornaments	*stylized decorative patterns*	12

Within each of these groups, the doodles were categorised by how many of the following features they contained: Stereotypy [endless repetition], 30%; Ornamental detail, 60%; Figures, 38%; Animals, 35%; Objects, 55%; Faces, 60%; Movement, 16%; Numbers, 37%; and Writing, 60%.

Some Australian restaurants in the 1930s provided menus with extra white space to encourage diners to doodle upon the cards rather than their tablecloths. Doodling is also an old term for playing the bagpipes, which were known as 'doodle-sacks'.

——————— JAMES BOND vs HUGO DRAX ———————

In Ian Fleming's novel *Moonraker* (1955), Sir Hugo Drax is suspected of cheating at bridge in the exclusive Mayfair club Blades. James Bond is called in by M to see whether these suspicions are true since, as M warns, 'cheating at cards can still smash a man. In so-called Society, it's about the only crime that can still finish you'. Bond quickly ascertains that Drax is indeed a cheat who places his silver cigarette-case on the baize to act as a 'Shiner' reflecting the cards as he

```
                    BOND
            ♦ Q, 8, 7, 6, 5, 4, 3, 2
              ♣ A, Q, 10, 8, 4
  DRAX                            MEYER
♠ A, K, Q, J              ♠ 6, 5, 4, 3, 2
♥ A, K, Q, J             ♥ 10, 9, 8, 7, 2
♦ A, K                        ♦ J, 10, 9
♣ K, J, 9
                     M
              ♠ 10, 9, 8, 7
               ♥ 6, 5, 4, 3
              ♣ 7, 6, 5, 3, 2
```

deals. Bond decides to humiliate Drax by switching the packs and dealing a rigged hand. Bond credits the hand to the bridge player Ely Culbertson (1891–1955), though it is probably a version of the famous whist hand which lost the Duke of Cumberland (1721–65) a reported bet of £20,000.

─────────── BECKHAM'S BODY ART ───────────

David Beckham has, to date, the following tattoos inked upon his body:

Back of neck........winged cross	Left forearm. *Ut Amem et Foveam*[2]
Lower back..............*Brooklyn*	Right forearm ....*VII*
Down spine........guardian angel	Right forearm. *Perfectio in Spiritu*[3]
Between shoulders ....*Romeo*	Right triceps......angel, with text
Left forearm ....*Victoria*[1]	*In the face of adversity*

[1] His wife's name is written in Hindi. Some have rather churlishly pointed out that it may contain a spelling mistake. [2] 'So that I love and cherish'. [3] 'Spiritual perfection'.

─────────── OXBRIDGE BLUES SPORTS ───────────

The first Oxford *vs* Cambridge Varsity match seems to have been a 2-day cricket match held at Lord's in 1827 (it was a draw). Two years later, the first boat race at Henley cemented the Oxbridge sporting rivalry. However, it was only with the second boat race in 1836 that the tradition was set of Oxford wearing dark blue and Cambridge wearing light blue (Cambridge, in fact, wear Eton blue). Nowadays, both universities award Blues, Half Blues, and Discretionary Blues each year to those who participate in the Varsity match of a variety of sports – although the institutions have slightly different criteria as to which sports they award Blues – and the awarding of Blues often differs between men and women. The table on the right indicates the current status of Full Blue sports:

Full Blue sport	O♂	O♀	C♂	C♀
Football	*	*	*	*
Athletics	*	*	*	*
Basketball	*	*	*	
Boat race	*		*	
Boxing	*		*	
Cricket	*		*	
Cross country	*	*	*	
Golf	*	*	*	
Hockey	*	*	*	*
Lawn tennis	*	*	*	*
Rugby Union	*	*	*	*
Squash	*	*	*	*
Swimming	*	*	*	*
Yachting	*	*		
Dancesport		*		
Fencing		*		
Karate		*		
Lacrosse		*		*
Modern pentathlon		*		*
Netball		*		*
Rowing		*		*

Half or Discretionary Blues can be awarded for a range of sports, including: American football, archery, badminton, ballroom dancing, basketball, boardsailing, canoe & kayak, chess, cricket, croquet, cross-country, cycling, Eton fives, fencing, gliding, gymnastics, ice hockey, Isis rowing, judo, karate, korfball, lacrosse, life saving, lightweight rowing, orienteering, pistol shooting, polo, power lifting, racquets, real tennis, riding, rifle shooting, rugby fives, rugby league, sailing, skiing, table tennis, tae kwon do, trampolining, ultimate frisbee, volleyball, water polo, weightlifting, and windsurfing.

———————— THE PAMPLONA BULL RUN ————————

Pamplona is the ancient Basque city in northern Spain famed for the annual 'running of the bulls', which takes place 7–14 July as part of the festival celebrating St Fermin – the city's patron saint. The purpose of the run is to transfer to the bullring each morning the six bulls which will fight that afternoon. For centuries, hundreds of foolhardy folk have dared to run along the narrow streets in front of the bulls – the aim being to see how close one can get to the animals without being trampled or gored to death. Runners must enter the fenced area of the run by 7·30am, after which they sing a song three times – at 7·55am, 7·57am, and 7·59am:

A San Fermín pedimos, por ser nuestro patrón, nos guíe en el encierro, dándonos su bendición	*We ask for San Fermin, who is our Patron, to guide us through the Bull Run, and give us his blessing.*

Then, at precisely 8·00am a rocket is launched to announce that the gates of the *Santo Domingo* enclosure [A] are open; a second rocket indicates that all the bulls have left the enclosure and are running down *Santo Domingo* [B] towards the the *Plaza Consistorial* [C]. A sharp turn takes the bulls up *Mercaderes* towards [D] where they turn into the long and narrow *Estafeta*. The bulls tend to slow down along this section until they exit the street [E], and enter the fenced funnel, *Teléfonica* [F], which herds them up the narrow *Callejón* [G] and into the *Plaza de Toros* [H]. A third rocket indicates all the bulls have entered the bullring, and a final rocket is fired when the event is over. The 825m run lasts, on average, just 4 minutes.

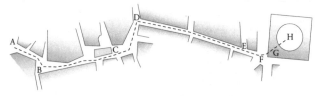

The popularity of the bull run is hard to fathom, especially since injury and death are not uncommon. The city of Pamplona advises that 'runners need to be calm people with good reflexes and in excellent physical shape' – though since 1910 at least thirteen have been killed during the run.

———————— CHECKMATE ————————

The term *checkmate*, used in chess to describe the position where a King cannot escape from an attack, literally means 'your King is dead' and it derives from the Arabic (and Persian) words: *shah* (king) and *mat* (dead).

WALKING DEFINED

The definition of walking for the purposes of racing is set down by the International Association of Athletic Federations (IAAF) in Rule 230.1:

Race Walking is a progression of steps so taken that the walker makes contact with the ground, so that no visible (to the human eye) loss of contact occurs. The advancing leg shall be straightened (i.e. not bent at the knee) from the moment of first contact with the ground until the vertical upright position.

Given the difficulty of maintaining these strict requirements over a long distance, disqualifications are not uncommon. For example, at the 2000 Sydney Olympics, Janet Saville was 150m away from a gold medal in the 20km walk when an Italian official issued her with a red card for 'lifting'.

GOLF STROKE NOMENCLATURE

Ace	hole in one	Par	0
Deuce	hole in two	Birdie	-1
Double Bogey	+2	Eagle	-2
Bogey	+1	Double Eagle, Albatross	-3

Until the 1940s or so, the term Bogey was used in the same way as Par, i.e. the 'scratch' number, or the number of strokes a good player ought to take on a hole. (Curiously, this number used also to be known as The Colonel, after a fictional military type who 'laid down the law'). Later, perhaps because of American influence, Bogey came to mean a stroke over Par. The Par of a hole usually depends on its length: usually Par 3, <250yds; Par 4, 251–475yds; Par 5, >476yds. The etymology of Birdie is a little unclear, though it might derive from old American slang where a 'bird' was anything pure, exceptional, or smart. It can safely be assumed that the use of Eagle and Albatross came about simply because they were more impressive birds. (Some players highlight Birdies on their scorecard with a circle, and Eagles with a square.) In the C19th, another set of terms was used to describe the number of strokes one had taken in relation to one's adversary. If your opponent had played one stroke more than you – known as 'the odds' – your next stroke would be 'the like'; if they had played two strokes more – that is, 'the two more' – your next stroke would be 'the one off two'; if three more, 'the one off three', and so on. One definition of a golfer is someone who shoots a five, shouts *Fore!*, and cards a three.

TYPES OF SNOOKER

The cue ball is SNOOKERED when it is obstructed from the path of the object ball by another ball. A CHINESE SNOOKER occurs when the cue ball has a clear line to the object ball, but cuing is hampered by another ball immediately behind the white. The cueball is said to be ANGLED when its path to the object ball is obstructed by the corner of a cushion.

—————————— SOME PARLOUR GAMES ——————————

The game of HESTIA involves two of a party secretly agreeing on a word which has various meanings, and then discussing the word in conversation in its various forms. Other members of the group may only join in when they think they have figured out the mystery word. For example, the word 'hare' might be talked about in the following way: 'Does yours run very fast?', 'No, but it grows quickly.' 'Is it brown?', 'Surely you can see that it is going grey!' – and so on until all but one player has twigged. The variant NEW HESTIA sees the word agreed by all of the group except one player who must guess from listening to the banter.

The timeless game of mental mathematical agility, FIZZ BUZZ, demands that all the players take turns in counting up from 1, substituting the word *fizz* for any multiple of 3, and *buzz* for any multiple of 5. If a number is a multiple of both 3 and 5 then *fizz buzz* is called. So, counting would start: '1, 2, *fizz*, 4, *buzz*, *fizz*, 7, 8, *fizz*, *buzz*, 11, *fizz*, 13, 14, *fizz buzz*, 16…' and so on. Of course, after this things get a little tricky.

The game of DUMB CRAMBO involves each player acting out a series of words which rhyme with the word they have been set, until that word is guessed by the rest of their team. For example, a player set the word 'tie' might act out the words 'die', 'spy', 'fly', 'fry', and so on, until 'tie' is correctly guessed.

The invention of the Post-It note has greatly facilitated the playing of FOREHEAD DETECTIVE. Here, each member of a group is allocated a famous character by the person on their left who writes the name on a piece of paper and appends it to the victim's forehead so that while they cannot see the name, it is visible to the rest of the group. Each player then takes it in turn to ask yes/no questions about their character until they are able to identify them.

In the lovely word-game LONDON UNDERGROUND players take it in turns to describe stations on the London tube network for other players to decode, for example:

Fabricated from beer…Maida Vale
Vicar's envy………Parsons Green
Burnt BBQ…………Blackfriars
Additional heath……Moor Park
Let pig decay……Turnham Green
Fill up a shop…………Stockwell
Larger lair for thieves……Morden
(Of course, this game can be played with any underground network or, indeed, any mutually agreed geography. Compare this game with *Mornington Crescent* on p.153.)

The SIMMONDS'S CAT is just one of many alphabet games. Players take it in turn to name an adjective to describe the Simmonds's cat – the initial letter of the adjective rotates through the alphabet. 'The Simmonds's cat is an *artful* cat'; '… a *belligerent* cat'; '… a *cheerful* cat'. A requirement for speed can be introduced into the game for more competitive players.

———————— SOME PARLOUR GAMES cont. ————————

In the game ADVERBS, while one player has left the room, each of the others selects their own adverb (e.g. *stupidly, clumsily, cheerfully*). The excluded player asks each person to perform an action (e.g. tying a shoelace, reading from a newspaper, &c.) in the manner of their adverb. The excluded player is allowed 3 guesses at each adverb.

At the start of the spelling game GHOSTS each player has 3 lives. The first player proposes a letter to which each subsequent player (in turn) has to add another letter. Any player who, by adding a letter, completes a word (longer than 3 letters) loses a life. Any player who is challenged and cannot propose a legitimate word they were 'aiming for', loses a life. Any player who makes a challenge which is shown to be unfounded loses a life. When a player has lost all of their lives they become a 'ghost', unable to propose letters, but able to harry and make misleading suggestions. If a ghost succeeds in tricking another player into losing a life, they are then reconstituted into living players of the game. Expert players who tire of the basic game can play REVERSE GHOSTS where words are spelled backwards.

REVERSE BOTTLETOP SPILLIKINS is played with a box of matches and a wine bottle. Players take it in turn to balance a match on the top of the wine bottle – the player who disturbs any of the matches so that it falls is deemed the loser.

The game WHAT'S WRONG? is a simple test of observation. All players but one are sent out of a room and, in their absence, a number of changes are made to the room's organisation (e.g. the clock is advanced an hour; a picture is moved or replaced, &c.). After a few minutes the others in the party return and have to write down what they think has been changed. Whomsoever identifies the most changes made to the room wins.

A number of parlour games can be played with a feather. FEATHER FLIGHT involves trying to keep a feather aloft by blowing – anyone who touches the feather is out. FEATHER FOOTBALL requires two teams on either side of a table. The aim is to blow the feather into the other team's half so that it touches either an opposing player, or so that it falls on the opposition's side of the table.

CHARACTER ASSASSINATION is best played with a group of close friends or relatives. With one person out of the room, the remaining players swap identities with one another. The excluded player must identify who is who by posing a set of questions or setting a series of tasks. The game may be expanded by including characters who are not actually present but are familiar to all.

[For a selection of forfeits which may be employed with these games, turn to p.136. For the ultimate parlour game, see the alleged death of Palmerston on p.44.]

TIPS FOR CONJURORS

Advice from *The Magician's Handbook* (1902) by 'Selbit' – a pseudonym of Percy Thomas Tibbles – who petulantly warns: '[if these] rules are not attended to, do not forget that you were well advised to remember them.'

1. When you enter the drawing room to do your show, do not go round and shake hands with the company. This might be taken for a piece of undue familiarity.

2. Do not say that if a trick is not properly applauded you will not continue your show. This would be considered a little out of place.

3. Presuming that you are doing a card trick and that a lady will not select the card you are attempting to force, do not swear at her. Swearing is not considered polite in Society.

4. When a bald-headed gentleman resents your producing eggs and cigars from his pate, do not tell him to keep his hair on.

5. If you bungle a trick and the audience notice it, do not explain the mistake by saying that you must be a fool. Possibly they might fall in with your belief.

6. Do not call the parlour-maid pet names or engage her in conversation to the neglect of your hostess. Remember that you are getting a free meal and that it is your duty to listen to ladies talking.

SCORING DIVING

The FINA judging of Olympic diving is a complex procedure. The dives themselves are judged subjectively on execution alone using these criteria:

0 points	*completely failed*	5–6	*satisfactory*
0·5–2	*unsatisfactory*	6·5–8	*good*
2·5–4·5	*deficient*	8·5–10	*very good*

Traditionally, seven judges present their scores, the highest and lowest marks are discarded, and the remaining scores are added together. This number is then multiplied by the dive's 'degree of difficulty' (DD) which is calculated by adding together the scores for the following five criteria:

A – somersaults · B – flight position · C – twists
D – approach group (e.g. armstands)
E – unnatural entry (e.g. reverse or armstand forwards)

Divers are therefore able to gamble the chance of a high execution score on a easier dive, with a lower execution score on a more convoluted dive.

PASCAL ON ENNUI

Nothing is as unbearable to man as to be completely at rest, without passion, without business, without diversion, without employment. This is when he feels his nothingness, his deprivation, his insufficiency, his dependency, his impotence, his hollowness. Presently, and from the depths of his soul he will bring up ennui, blackness, sadness, grief, resentment, despair.

— BLAISE PASCAL, *Pensées*, 1670

THE OFFSIDE RULE: AN ELEMENTARY GUIDE

In football, a player is offside if he is nearer to his opponent's goal than both the ball and the second to last opponent. However, a player cannot be offside if [a] they are in their own half; or [b] they are level with the second last or last two opponents. Moreover, being in an offside position is not an offence in itself. A player can only be penalised for being offside if, at the moment the ball is played forwards by a team-mate, the player is (in the opinion of the referee) involved in 'active play'. This means: [a] interfering with play; [b] interfering with an opponent; or [c] gaining advantage by being in the offside position. Recently FIFA have attempted to modify the interpretation of 'active play' to encourage more attacking football. For example, 'interfering with play' is to be interpreted as playing or touching a ball passed or touched by a team-mate, and 'interfering with an opponent' is to include obstructing the goalkeeper's line of vision, or making distracting or deceiving gestures. Offside players can also be penalised if they are deemed to have gained an advantage by playing a ball that has rebounded off a post or a crossbar, or one that has rebounded off an opponent. Three offside illustrations are given below:

offside

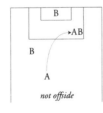

not offside

offside

However, players cannot be penalised for being offside in any event if they receive a ball directly from a goal kick, a throw-in, or a corner kick. The penalty for any offside infringement is the award of a free kick to the opposing team – taken from the spot where the infringement occurred.

FORTUNE-TELLER FOLDING

Take a square sheet of paper, and fold each corner in half to mark the centre[1]. Fold each corner into the centre [2] to form a smaller square and turn the paper over [3].

Fold each corner into the centre [4] and crease the square across its centre (vertically and horizontally) [5]. Fold the paper in half and turn it over [6]. Tuck your thumbs and first fingers under the four square flaps [7] and push upwards and outwards.

Under the innermost flaps scribble a set of appropriate predictions ('you fancy Miss Thomas'); annotate the inside flaps with numbers; and decorate the outside flaps with colours. Ask the victim to pick a colour from the outer flap and, with your fingers under the flaps (as in 7), open and close the folder, vertically and horizontally in turn, once for each letter in the colour chosen. Then, with the folder open at the appropriate place, ask the victim to pick one of the visible numbers. Open and close the folder as many times as the number picked. Ask the victim to choose another of the visible numbers; lift the corresponding flap and reveal their future.

MEXICAN WAVES

Although 'Mexican waves' – the undulating effect of a crowd of spectators jumping to their feet and waving their hands in the air like they just don't care – have long been part of stadia entertainment, the term was only coined during the 1986 World Cup in Mexico City. Research into these waves (known also as *La Ola* by Illés Farkas et al. [*Nature* 2002; 419:131–2] indicates that waves usually move in a clockwise direction at an average speed of 12m (*c.*20 seats) per second. They tend to be 6–12m (*c.*15 seats) wide, and can be instigated by only a few dozen spectators. Mexican waves at Lord's (the spiritual home of cricket) circle the ground but cease temporarily between the Allen and Warner Stands while the wave passes invisibly through the MCC Members' seats in the Pavilion. The restraint of the Members is usually accompanied by a humorous chorus of boos.

———————— SQUASH BALL COLOURINGS ————————

Squash balls (whatever their overall colour) are usually coded with a coloured dot which indicates how fast they will travel. As a general rule of thumb, better players will use slower balls, and amateurs faster ones:

Super slow ..	(Double) Yellow Dot	Medium	Red Dot
Slow	White or Green Dot	Fast	Blue Dot

Competitions held under the auspices of the World Squash Federation are played with Yellow Dot (or Double Yellow Dot) balls, the slowest available, which must conform to a set of precise technical specifications:

Weight	24g (±1)
Diameter	40mm (±0·5) [*larger balls may be permitted*]
Stiffness	3·2 (N/mm @ 23ºC) (±0·4)
Rebound resilience – from 254cm @ 23ºC	>12%
Rebound resilience – from 254cm @ 45ºC	26–33%

———————————— SHOOTING NUMBERS ————————————

In shooting terminology two birds is a BRACE and three birds is a LEASH.

———————— DUCKS, DRAKES, RAMS, AND EWES ————————

'Ducks and Drakes' is the gentle art of skimming stones across the surface of a calm pond or river – the aim being to ricochet a stone across the water as many times as possible before it sinks. Smooth, flat stones and shells are the ideal ammunition for this sport, as the poet Butler notes:

What figured slates are best to make, On watery surface duck and drake
— SAMUEL BUTLER, *Hudibras*, ii 3

Some British enthusiasts keep score of the number of bounces achieved by employing the terms shepherds traditionally used to count their sheep:

1 .... Yan	8 .... Overa	15 .... Bumfit
2 .... Tan	9 .... Covera	16 ...... Yan-a-Bumfit
3 .... Tether	10 .... Dicks	17 ..... Tan-a-Bumfit
4 .... Mether	11 .... Yan-a-Dicks	18 ... Tether-a-Bumfit
5 .... Pit	12 .... Tan-a-Dicks	19 .. Mether-a-Bumfit
6 .... Tayter	13 .... Tether-a-Dicks	20 .... Jiggit
7 .... Layter	14 ... Mether-a-Dicks	(*20 sheep are a 'score'*)

─── DICKENS'S DISTINCTION OF IDLERS ───

Mr Thomas Idle and Mr Francis Goodchild … were both idle in the last degree. Between Francis and Thomas, however, there was this difference of character: Goodchild was laboriously idle, and would take upon himself any amount of pains and labour to assure himself that he was idle; in short had no better idea of idleness than that it was useless industry. Thomas Idle, on the other hand, was an idler of the unmixed Irish or Neapolitan type; a passive idler, a born-and-bred idler, a consistent idler, who practised what he would have preached if he had not been too idle to preach; a one entire and perfect chrysolite of idleness.

— *The Lazy Tour of Two Idle Apprentices*, 1857

───THE UNLIKELY INVENTION OF CHESS───

John de Vigney, author of *The Moralisation of Chess*, asserted (somewhat bizarrely) that a philosopher called Xerxes invented the game of chess under the Babylonian King Evil-Merodach (*c.*?6BC) in the following way:

There are three reasons which induced the philosopher to introduce this new pastime: the first, to reclaim a wicked king; the second, to prevent idleness; and the third, practically to demonstrate the nature and necessity of nobleness.

─── FOCAL DYSTONIA, CHOKING, & THE YIPS ───

The 'yips' are the involuntary and uncontrolled jerks, tremors, or freezing which affect certain individuals when they undertake finely controlled motor skills. In the world of sport, where fine movements can assume critical importance, the yips are most often associated with golf, especially putting or chipping, when a sudden jerk of the wrist can send a ball whizzing past the cup. According to Smith et al. [*Sports Med.* 2003;33:13 –31] yips-affected golfers add approximately 4·7 strokes to their scores over 18 holes. However, the yips can also affect a host of other sportsmen, including bowlers, snooker players, darts throwers, and even petanque chuckers. Considerable research has been undertaken into the yips, with some neurological evidence suggesting that they may be a form of focal dystonia. Such task-specific dystonias affect groups of muscles, usually when placed under repeated stress, and they include the commonly suffered 'writer's cramp'. The controversial suggestion that psychological factors like 'performance anxiety' or 'choking' might play a contributory part in such involuntary movements on the sports field is much disputed.

——————— 'ONE HELL OF A BEATING' ———————

Bjørge Lillelien's now infamous commentary on Norwegian television
after Norway beat England 2–1 in Oslo at a 1981 World Cup qualifier:

> *Lord Nelson! Lord Beaverbrook! Sir Winston Churchill!*
> *Sir Anthony Eden! Clement Attlee! Henry Cooper! Lady Diana!*
> *Maggie Thatcher! Can you hear me, Maggie Thatcher?*
> *Your boys took one hell of a beating!*
> *Your boys took one hell of a beating!*

——————— THE KNIGHT'S TOUR ———————

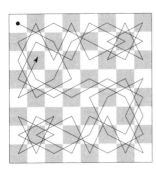

The Knight's Tour is a mathematical
chess puzzle, the aim of which is to
move a knight (as he moves in the
game of chess) 64 times so that he
rests once, and only once, on each
square. A 'perfect' solution is where
the knight finishes on a square one
move away from his starting point,
demonstrating that the tour could be
continued *ad infinitum*. The route
opposite by Monneron (*fl.*1776) is an
example of a perfect Knight's Tour.

——————— DOWN & OUT BOXING COUNTS ———————

In Olympic boxing, if a contestant is knocked down, the referee begins a
count of 10 seconds starting from 1 second after the boxer is considered
down. (If the opposing fighter does not move to a neutral corner, then the
referee will pause his count until he does so.) Once the referee has
counted 10 and called 'out', the bout ends as a 'knock-out'. In any case,
the round cannot resume until the referee has called 8, even if the downed
fighter is ready to continue. If the same boxer goes down again, without
having received a fresh blow, the referee continues his count from 8. If
both boxers go down together, counting continues for as long as one is
still down. A boxer is down if, as the result of a blow or series of blows:

> He touches the floor with any part of his body other than his feet
> He hangs helplessly on the ropes
> He is outside or partly outside the ropes
> He is in a semi-conscious state and cannot continue the bout

STONYHURST FOOTBALL

A kind of football played at Stonyhurst and some other schools. It differs materially from the Association and Rugby games, chiefly in these respects: (1) any number may play at once; (2) the ball may be touched by the hand during the game, but not handled or carried as in Rugby football; (3) charging, or otherwise roughly treating another player, is prohibited. The goal posts are longer and the space between them narrower than in any other form of the game; the ball is small and round. It is akin to a species of football played at Eton, and is clearly a relic of the past. In matches the sides usually have names: e.g. 'French *vs* English' in the Grand Matches – a significant survival from old continental days; 'Federals *vs* Allies' (now obsolete); 'Pipes *vs* Windows' – a favourite impromptu match, the 'Pipes' being those who sit on one side of the old Study Place, the 'Windows' those who sit on the other. Now that the pipes (hot water pipes) are on the same side as the windows, the match is more commonly called 'Walls *vs* Windows', but sometimes 'Chapel Pipes *vs* Windows'. 'Shavers *vs* Non-shavers' is another favourite competition.

— JOHN STEPHEN FARMER, *The Public School Word-Book*, 1900

A QUESTION OF SPORT

First broadcast at 6·20pm on Monday 5 January 1970, the BBC's *A Question of Sport* has, to date, had three hosts and twelve team captains:

HOSTS – David Vine · David Coleman · Sue Barker
TEAM CAPTAINS – Henry Cooper · David Coleman · Cliff Morgan
Fred Trueman · Willie Carson · Emlyn Hughes · Bill Beaumont
Ian Botham · John Parrott · Ally McCoist · Frankie Dettori

WOMEN & THE OLYMPIC MOVEMENT

Although the Olympic movement likes to present itself as inclusive and meritocratic, this was not always the case. The 'father' of the modern Olympics, Pierre de Coubertin (see also p.71), had opposed the inclusion of females at the Games, stating 'Olympics with women would be incorrect, unpractical, uninteresting and unaesthetic'. An early IOC statement on the question declared, 'We feel that the Olympic Games must be reserved for the solemn and periodic exaltation of male athleticism with internationalism as a base, loyalty as a means, arts for its setting, and female applause as its reward.' In 1900 the floodgates opened, and 11 women (against 1319 men) were permitted to compete at tennis and golf.

— CLUEDO CHARACTERS, WEAPONS, & ROOMS —

The tense board game *Cluedo* (called *Clue* in the US) is initiated by the murder of Dr Black (Mr John Boddy in the US) by one of the following:

Col. Mustard .. yellow	Rev. Green...... green	Miss Scarlett ...... red
Prof. Plum..... purple	Mrs Peacock ..... blue	Mrs White...... white

The murder weapons, and the rooms in which they are first located, are:

Dagger .... ballroom	Rope....................... lounge
Lead piping .... conservatory	Candlestick.......... dining room
Revolver .... study	Spanner.................... kitchen

Simpsons' Cluedo, set in Springfield, is premised on Chief Wiggum's investigation into the murder of wizened plutocrat Monty Burns. The suspects are: Homer, Marge, Lisa, Bart, Krusty the Clown, and Waylon Smithers. (Lisa Simpson, as Miss Scarlett, plays first.) The murder weapons are: the poisoned donut, the Extend-O-Glove, a necklace, a slingshot, a rod of plutonium, and a saxophone. The nine locations are: Barney's Bowl-A-Rama, Burns Manor, the Simpson house, Krustylu Studios, the nuclear power plant, the Frying Dutchman, Springfield Retirement Castle, the Android's Dungeon, & the Kwik-E-Mart.

— SURF HEIGHT MEASUREMENT —

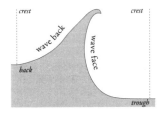

Traditionally, Hawaiian surfers used to measure the height of waves from the back to the crest. However, since the rest of the world employs the Wave Face as the standard measure, the 'Hawaiian Scale' (which tended to understate Face height by ⅓–½†) has fallen out of common usage.

wave face (ft) description	4–5 ...... waist–chest	7–10.. overhead & ½
0–1 .... foot–ankle	5–6....... chest–head	10–15 .... double o/h
2–3...... knee–waist	6–7.. head–overhead	15–20...... triple o/h

† Although there is some debate as to the origin of the Hawaiian wave measure, it seems to be part of an inverse machismo, whereby surfers underestimated the waves they rode.

— THE HABIT OF SNOOKER —

Playing snooker gives you firm hands and helps to build up character. It is the ideal recreation for dedicated nuns.

— ARCHBISHOP LUIGI BARBARITO, *Apostolic Nuncio Emeritus*, 1989

TICK TACK or TIC TAC

Tick Tack men (or, as they used to be known, 'racecourse telegraphists' or 'arm-swingers') employ a complex series of hand signals to communicate to their colleagues the racing odds of horses or dogs (see also p.42). Some of these splendid signals (taken from the Piney System) are illustrated below:

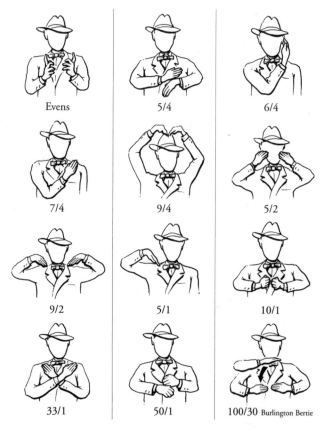

Evens	5/4	6/4
7/4	9/4	5/2
9/2	5/1	10/1
33/1	50/1	100/30 Burlington Bertie

Punters should be warned that the white-gloved Tick Tackers are far too canny to employ a code which just anyone could decipher. Not only do Tick Tack codes vary, but each firm of bookmakers will use (and regularly change) a 'twist card' which jumbles the odds. So, for example, when a racecourse telegraphist is signalling 100/30, they might really mean 5/4.

GOLF GRAND-SLAM EVENTS

Masters (April) · US Open (June) · British Open (July) · PGA (August)

CAMBRIDGE NIGHT CLIMBING

The Night Climbers of Cambridge was published pseudonymously in 1937 by 'Whipplesnaith' (possibly Noël Howard Symington). It has long been rumoured that the book was 'restricted' by the Cambridge University Library not only because it incited undergraduates to climb the historic monuments of the town by night, but also because it gave them detailed instructions on how to do so. The book explains the two basic variations on the climbing landscape (the drainpipe and the chimney), and details some of the more interesting routes. Climbing onto the Old Library on Senate House Passage is regarded as a beginner's climb which provides such 'genteel' access to King's College that it is ideal for a reveller 'should he be in evening dress'. A nearby route involves climbing up the South face of Gonville & Caius, and leaping about seven foot onto the roof of Senate House. Other routes detailed by Whipplesnaith include the face of the Fitzwilliam Museum; the main gate of St John's; the Bridge of Sighs; the north face of Pembroke; Trinity Library; the south-east corner of Clare; and, of course, King's Chapel. 'There is probably no building in the world which has aroused such interest among climbers as King's Chapel ... it has a fascination about it which will not let the mind rest.' Whipplesnaith describes in detail the various stages of the climb, from how to get into King's in the first place, to the pros and cons of using the lightning conductor. It seems that between the Wars, the roof of King's Chapel was abuzz with climbers – as *The Times* noted on 25 May 1932:

> FLAG & BOTTLE ON CAMBRIDGE COLLEGE CHAPEL
> *Roof climbers were again busy at King's College Chapel, Cambridge, on Monday night and fastened a full-size Union Jack on the north-east pinnacle of the building. From that pinnacle to the centre pinnacle a wire was slung from which is now suspended a bottle of wine. The umbrella fastened on the pinnacle on the other side is still there, though in a very bedraggled condition.*

Of course, since most of the buildings described in *The Night Climbers of Cambridge* are preserved by Grade I listed status, the book remains useful.

SNAKES & LADDERS

On a traditional 10 x 10 board there are twelve snakes and eight ladders.

──── FRENCH PLAYING-CARD CHARACTERS ────

Considerable speculation surrounds the identities of the 12 Court cards in the traditional French playing-card pack. One possible explanation is:

Suit	King	Queen	Knave
Spades	David (Jewish)	Pallas (wisdom)	Ogier
Clubs	Alexander (Greek)	Judith (fortitude)	Lancelot
Diamonds	Caesar (Roman)	Rachael (piety)	Hector
Hearts	Charlemagne (Frankish)	Juno (royalty)	La Hire

──── MORRIS DANCES ────

Dating back to at least the C15th, morris dancing is a traditional form of folk entertainment which may owe its origins to ancient fertility cults. Many of the folk songs and dances which still survive were preserved by Cecil Sharp, who began collecting music and dances in 1899. Most modern morris dances involve men (and nowadays women) dressed in white outfits decorated with rosettes, flowers, ribbons, and bells, carrying handkerchiefs, sticks, or inflated pigs' bladders. Some of the dances are:

STICK DANCES · Dancers carry a short stick in their right hand which are rhythmically clashed. E.g. *Bean-setting, Lads a Bunchum, Vandalls of Hammerwich, Rodney.*

HANDKERCHIEF DANCES · White hankies are held in both hands, between forefinger and thumb, so they gently billow as the dance is performed. E.g. *Country Gardens, Bobbing Joe, Laudnum Bunches.*

LINKED HANDKERCHIEFS · Here handkerchiefs are held between pairs and used to create tunnels and suchlike. E.g. *The old woman who carried a broom.*

CORNER DANCES · Where pairs take it in turns to dance while the other pairs look on. E.g. *Trunkles, The old frog dance, How d'ye do, sir?*

PROCESSIONAL DANCES · Usually performed as part of a forward-moving procession. E.g. *Bonny Green Garters.*

MORRIS JIGS · Generally a solo dance where other dancers mimic the actions of the first. E.g. *Lumps of plum pudding, The Nutting Girl.*

The most infamous and oft repeated remark on this form of activity is: 'You should make a point of trying every experience once, excepting incest and morris dancing.' Over the years, the quotation has been attributed to a wealth of individuals, including Sir Thomas Beecham, Sir Malcolm Sargent, Noël Coward, and Sir Arnold Bax (quoting 'a sympathetic Scot'). It was even repeated in the House of Lords by Lord McIntosh of Haringey. The quote has been used as the title of a splendid book on British food by Jonathan Meades, as well as the curious autobiography of, er, 'model' Linzi Drew.

ON JUGGLERS

The profession of the juggler, with that of the minstrel, had fallen so low in the public estimation at the close of the reign of Queen Elizabeth, that the performers were ranked, by the moral writers of the time, not only with 'ruffians, blasphemers, thieves, and vagabonds'; but also with 'Heretics, Jews, Pagans, and sorcerers'. In more modern times, by way of derision, the juggler was called a hocus-pocus, a term applicable to a pick-pocket or a common cheat.

— JOSEPH STRUTT, *Sports & Pastimes of the People of England,* 1801

FOOTBALL LINE DECISIONS

ROCKY'S FIGHTS

MOVIE	OPPONENT	OUTCOME
Rocky (1976)	Apollo Creed[1]	*Creed wins on split decision – 15R*
Rocky II (1979)	Apollo Creed	*Rocky wins – KO 15R*
Rocky III (1982)	Clubber Lang[2]	*Rocky loses – KO 2R*
		rematch; Rocky wins – KO 3R
Rocky IV (1985)	Ivan Drago[3]	*Rocky wins – KO 15R*
Rocky V (1990)	Tommy Gunn[4]	*Rocky defeats the punk in a street fight*

Sylvester Stallone wrote all five *Rocky* films himself after being inspired by a fight between 'nobody' Chuck Wepner and Muhammad Ali, in which Wepner, to everyone's astonishment, lasted the full fifteen rounds. The first *Rocky* film won the Academy Award for Best Picture (beating *All The President's Men* and *Taxi Driver*) and Sylvester Stallone himself was nominated for Best Actor. [1] Apollo Creed was played by Carl Weathers. [2] Clubber Lang was played by the legendary Mr T. During the film he utters the immortal line *'No, I don't hate Balboa. I pity the fool!'.* [3] Ivan Drago was played by Dolph Lundgren. *Rocky IV* portrays a Cold War grudge match prompted by Russian Ivan Drago killing American Apollo Creed. After beating Drago, Rocky makes a toe-curling anti-Cold War speech, encouraging friendship and understanding between the two countries. [4] Tommy Gunn was played by Tommy Morrison.

RUNNING THE MILE

The mile was originally a Roman unit of 1,000 paces (roughly 1,618 yds), but since then it has varied widely across countries and cultures. In 1592 the Statute Mile [Act 35 Eliz.I, c.6, s.8] was defined as 8 furlongs of 40 16-foot poles, or 1,760 yards – a definition which still stands. For many years it was assumed that a sub-four-minute mile was beyond the scope of human achievement. Yet as athletics grew in popularity during the C19th, and sophisticated watches were able to record minute fractions of time, so the hunger to break this theoretical barrier intensified. During the 1930s, 40s, and 50s, seconds were gradually chipped off the mile and, on the 6 May 1954, Roger Bannister managed to record the time of 3:59·4.

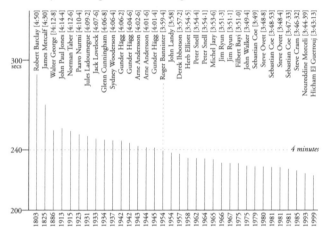

Although Bannister's record lasted only 46 days, it was clear as soon as his time was announced that the run had been something unique. As the London *Times* reported the following day: 'Bannister's performance … will earn for him athletic immortality no matter how soon someone else goes a fraction of a second better – or even a shade better than that.'

GOLFING HONOUR

The 'honour' at a golf tee (i.e. the player who tees-off first) is decided at the first hole by drawing lots. Thereafter, the player who scores the lowest on each hole has the honour at the next tee. If the scores are tied, then whoever had the honour at the previous hole tees off first at the next. During a game, the ball farthest from the hole is the first to be played.

PILATES

German-born Joseph Hubertus Pilates (1880–1967) pioneered a system of exercises to develop and enhance strength, posture, and flexibility which he called CONTROLOGY. Pilates was a sickly child who from an early age studied anatomy to build up his body. He travelled to England in 1912 (apparently to work as a circus performer), but two years later, at the start of WWI, was interned as an enemy alien. While in the camps Pilates found work as a nurse and experimented with a range of techniques and makeshift equipment to rehabilitate the immobile. On his release, he used these skills to help train the German police force before emigrating to New York in 1925 and setting up a gym. Since then, the techniques of Pilates have been adopted across the world, and are used by a host of athletes, dancers, actors, sportsmen and women, as well as the infirm.

MUSCLE

40–50% of the human body consists of muscle – contractile tissue which is able to initiate or sustain movement. Three basic types of muscle exist:

SKELETAL... *under voluntary control; usually attatched to bone via tendons*
SMOOTH . *not under voluntary control; occurs in the gut, blood vessels, &c.*
CARDIAC...................... *occurs only in the heart; beats rhythmically*

CROSSWORD SETTERS & THE INQUISITION

Many setters of cryptic crosswords are keen to shroud their devilish work under the cloak of secrecy. To maintain consistency and shun the cult of personality, crosswords in *The Times* have always been anonymous. In contrast, the highly respected crossword editor of the *Guardian*, John Perkin, introduced pseudonyms to identify different setters 'both as a promise and a warning to the readers'. Among the most celebrated of setters is Edward Powys Mather, who worked for the *Observer* between 1926–39 as TORQUEMADA – a reference to Tomás de Torquemada, the first inquisitor-general of the Spanish Inquisition. Mather was succeeded by Derrick Macnutt, who worked until 1972 as XIMENES – a reference to another inquisitor-general, Cardinal Francisco Ximénes de Cisneros. When Jonathan Crowther took over, he chose the pseudonym AZED, which is both a pun on the alphabet, and an anagram of yet a third inquisitor-general, Diego de Deza. One of the best-loved compilers is John Graham, who writes for the *Guardian* as ARAUCARIA, and for the *Financial Times* as CINEPHILE. (*Araucaria* is the monkey-puzzle tree; and cinephile is an anagram of *chile pine*, another name for the *araucaria*.)

CASTING HAND SHADOWS

Pig

Dove

Elephant

The shadows of things are greater than themselves; and the more exaggerated the shadow, the more unlike the substance.
— HERMAN MELVILLE

Greyhound

Rabbit

Goat

Camel

Puppy

POLO CHUKKAS

The game of Polo is divided into *chukkas* of seven and a half minutes. At the end of each *chukka* a bell is rung, and the play is extended for thirty seconds unless the ball goes out of play, or the umpire calls a foul. [The last *chukka* of a match stops after seven minutes with no additional time added.] Between each *chukka* there is a three-minute interval – extended to five minutes at half-time. A full match lasts for six *chukkas*, but sometimes four or eight are played by mutual agreement. If, at the end of the final *chukka*, the scores are tied, then an interval of five minutes is called, the distance between the goals is widened from eight to sixteen yards, and additional *chukkas* are played until the deciding goal is scored. [The Oxford English Dictionary *gives the etymology of* chukka *as derived from the Hindustani* chakar *and the Sanskrit* cakra *meaning circle or wheel.*]

─────────── SIESTAS ───────────

One of the glories of idling is the *siesta* – a short nap in the middle of the day popular in and around the Mediterranean but cherished equally in countries across the world. The word derives from the Latin *sexta hora* – literally the sixth hour which, in most temperate countries, is likely to be the hottest. Perhaps because of dismal weather the English have tended to eschew the practice of snoozing during the day, as Noël Coward observed:

> Mad dogs and Englishmen go out in the midday sun,
> The Japanese don't care to, the Chinese wouldn't dare to
> Hindus and Argentines sleep firmly from twelve to one
> But Englishmen detest-a siesta.

─────────── THE HAKA ───────────

Many different types of *Haka* exist – and most Maori tribes have their own variation, some performed with weapons, others without. The *Haka* famously performed by the New Zealand Rugby team is called *Ka Mate*.

An introduction by the leader reminds the team how to conduct the Haka:

Ringa pakia	Slap your thighs
Uma tiraha	Puff out the chest
Turi Whatia	Bend the knees
Hope whai ake	Let the hip follow
Waewae takahia kia kino	Stamp the feet as hard as you can

The whole team then performs:

Ka mate! Ka mate!	It is death! It is death!
Ka ora! Ka ora!	It is life! It is life!
Ka mate! Ka mate!	It is death! It is death!
Ka ora! Ka ora!	It is life! It is life!
Tenei te tangata puhuru huru	This is the man above me
Nana i tiki mai	Who enabled me to live
Whakawhiti te ra	As I climb up
A hupane, kaupane	Step by step
A hupane, kaupane	Step by step
Whiti te ra!	Towards sunlight!

The first Haka ever danced overseas at a rugby match was that performed by the New Zealand Native team during their 1888–9 tour of Britain.
(A number of different translations for this Haka exist – some more belligerent than others.)

—SOME SPORTING, GAMING, & IDLING ON FILM—

❦ AMERICAN FOOTBALL · *Rudy*; *The Longest Yard*; *Knute Rockne* ['win one for the Gipper']; *North Dallas Forty* ❦ ARCHERY · *Deliverance* ['Goddamn, you play a mean banjo!'] ❦ AUTO RACING · *Grand Prix*; *Cannonball Run* ['God is our co-pilot!']; *Genevieve*; *Days of Thunder*; *Rebel Without a Cause* ❦ BASEBALL · *Bull Durham*; *The Natural*; *Bang The Drum Slowly*; *The Naked Gun*; *Pride of the Yankees*; *The Bad News Bears*; *Field of Dreams* ❦ BASKETBALL · *White Men Can't Jump* ['you either smoke or you get smoked']; *Hoop Dreams*; *Hoosiers* ❦ BOBSLED · *Cool Runnings*; *On Her Majesty's Secret Service* ❦ BOWLS · *Blackball* ❦ BOXING · *Raging Bull*; *Rocky* (see also p.35); *When We Were Kings* ['I'm so mean, I make medicine sick.']; *Ali* ❦ CARDS · *House of Games*; *The Cincinnati Kid* ['all you paid was the looking price. Lessons are extra']; *The Sting*; *Rounders*; *The Music of Chance* ❦ CHESS · *Casablanca*; *Blade Runner* (see p.119); *The Thomas Crown Affair*; *The Seventh Seal*†; *Harry Potter & the Philosopher's Stone* ❦ CYCLING · *Belleville Rendezvous*; *Breaking Away*; *American Flyers* ❦ CRICKET · *The Go-Between*; *Lagaan*; *Raffles*; *Wondrous Oblivion* ❦ FENCING · *Scaramouche*; *Hamlet*; *Die Another Day* ❦ FISHING · *A River Runs Through It*; *Jaws* ['You're gonna need a bigger boat']; *Big Fish*; *Grumpy Old Men* ❦ FOOTBALL · *Fever Pitch*; *Bend it Like Beckham*; *Escape to Victory* (see p.131); *Gregory's Girl* ❦ GOLF · *Tin Cup*; *Caddyshack* ['I won't be a caddy all my life. I'm going to carwash school in the fall']; *Goldfinger* (see p.120); *Happy Gilmore* ❦ HORSE RACING · *National Velvet*; *Bite the Bullet*; *Seabiscuit*; *The Killing* · ICE HOCKEY · *Slapshot*; *The Mighty Ducks*; *Miracle*; *Sudden Death* ❦ IDLING · *Ferris Bueller's Day Off* ['How could I possibly be expected to handle school on a day like this?']; *Withnail and I*; *Clerks*; *Barfly*; *Slackers*; *Waiting for Godot*; *Trainspotting*; *Smoke*; *High Fidelity*; *Mallrats*; *Swingers* ['You're so money, and you don't even know it!']; ❦ MARTIAL ARTS · *The Karate Kid* ['wax on, wax off!']; *Pink Panther* films ['Not now, Cato!']; *Enter the Dragon (&c.)* ❦ NIM · (see p.150) ❦ NOUGHTS & CROSSES ·*War Games* ['Greetings, Professor Falken'] ❦ OLYMPICS · *Olympia*; *Walk, Don't Run* ❦ POOL · *The Hustler* ['This is my table, man. I own it']; *The Color of Money* ❦ ROLLERBALL · *Rollerball* ❦ RUGBY · *This Sporting Life*; *Up 'n' Under* ❦ RUNNING · *Chariots of Fire*; *Loneliness of the Long Distance Runner* ❦ SAILING · *Swallows & Amazons*; *Knife in the Water*; *Dead Calm*; *Pirates of the Caribbean*; *The African Queen* ❦ SHOOTING · *The Shooting Party*; *Gosford Park* ❦ SNOOKER · *Sleuth* ['whatever are you doing with that cue in your hand, dear boy?'] ❦ SKIING · *Downhill Racer*; *Hot Dog* ❦ SPORTS' AGENTS · *Jerry Maguire* ['Show me the money!'] ❦ SURFING · *The Endless Summer*; *Big Wednesday*; *Point Break*; *Blue Crush*; *Crystal Voyager* ❦ TABLE TENNIS · *Forrest Gump*; *Ping Pong* ❦ TENNIS · *Monsieur Hulot's Holiday*; *School for Scoundrels*; *Pat and Mike*; *The Royal Tenenbaums*; *Strangers on a Train*; *Wimbledon* ❦ TENPIN BOWLING · *The Big Lebowski* ['You don't fool Jesus!']; *Kingpin*; *The Big Empty* ❦ TWISTER · *Bill & Ted's Bogus Journey*† ['Ted, don't fear the Reaper!'] ❦ † Both films feature games played against Death. ❦

KIPLING ON CHRISTMAS DAY SHOOTS

'Peace on Earth, Goodwill to men!'
So greet we Christmas Day.
Oh Christian load your gun and then,
Oh Christian, out and slay!

— RUDYARD KIPLING, *An Almanac of Twelve Sports*, 1898

SOME MATCHSTICK PUZZLES OF NOTE

[a] remove 8 matches
to form 2 squares

[c] remove 9 matches
to leave no squares

[e] remove 6 matches
to leave 2 squares

[f] remove 5 matches
to leave 3 squares

[b] move 4 matches
to form 3 squares

[d] remove 3 matches
to form 3 squares

[g] move 3 matches
to leave 4 squares

[See p.160 for solutions.]

RUGBY SCORING COMPARISON

RUGBY UNION†		RUGBY LEAGUE	
Try....................*points* 5		Try..........................*points* 4	
Dropped goal....................3		Dropped goal....................1	
Penalty goal.....................3		Penalty goal.....................2	
Conversion 2		Conversion 2	

† Points were first introduced in 1886 when a try was worth 1 and a converted try (a goal) was worth 3 – and if no goals were scored the match was declared a draw. In 1892 a try was worth 2 points, penalties and conversions were worth 3, dropped goals and field goals were worth 4. In 1905, the try was worth 3 points, the conversion was reduced to 2, and the field goal was abolished. In 1973 the try was worth 4 points, and in 1992 5 points.

BETTING ODDS SLANG

Evens	Levels, Scotch (see p.32)	7/1	Nevs
2/1	Bottle	8/1	T.H.
3/1	Carpet, Gimmel	9/1	Enin
4/1	Rouf	10/1	Cockle, Net
5/1	Hand	11/10	Tips
5/2	Face	33/1	Double Carpet
6/1	X's	100/30	Burlington Bertie (see p.101)

YAWNING

[a] grotesque display of a mouth opening to its maximal width, in association with a diaphragm contracting to an uncommon degree, expanding the lung for an excessive intake of air, aided by a spasmodic elevation of the pharynx blocking the customary gentle nasal airways

— DR FRANCIS SCHILLER, *J Hist Neurosci*, 2002;11:393

Contrary to popular belief, it seems likely that yawning (also oscitation, hiation, and pandiculation) has little to do with any need for extra oxygen in the lungs. Not only do we breathe in far more oxygen than we use (hence exhaled air contains oxygen), but ultrasound scans indicate that fetuses yawn *in utero* even though their lungs are not ventilated. Research by Steven Provine et al. [*Behav Neural Biol* 1987;48:382–93] that tested yawning in environments with high levels of both CO_2 and O_2 indicated that yawning 'does not serve a primary respiratory function and that yawning and breathing are triggered by different internal states and are controlled by separate mechanisms'. So, if we do not yawn because of so-called 'air hunger', why do we yawn at all? Many theories have been posited: that yawning raises brain power; that it serves to enhance our sense of smell; that we yawn when our state of alertness changes; that we yawn when we are plain bored; and so on. Indeed, if why we yawn is a mystery, so too is yawning's contagiousness. The French proverb 'one yawn will breed seven' is borne out by scientific studies as well as casual observation. (Aristotle noted that 'like a donkey urinates when he sees or hears another donkey do it, so also man yawns seeing someone else do it'.) It seems that yawning can be contagious if we see it, hear it, think of it, or read about it. Research, again by Provine, suggests that at least a quarter of those who read this entry will yawn as a result. Recent investigations have explored links between yawning and empathy, questioning whether yawning is more of a social, paralinguistic act than it is a physiological necessity – though nearly all of those who have written on the subject note how utterly satisfying and pleasing it is to stretch out fully and yawn deeply.

CONKERS

Conkers are the inedible nuts of the horse chestnut tree – one of a group of trees (notably *Aesculus hippocastanum*) with five-lobed (palmate) leaves and conical clusters of flowers. (In America, the trees are called Buckeyes.) As every school-boy knows, conkers are pierced with a skewer, and a length of string, twine, or shoelace, is threaded through the resulting hole. Players then alternate in striking at their opponent's conker, and the game ends either when one of the conkers is smashed, or when break-time is over. As might be expected from such an informal game, a number of variations exist. In some games each player takes three shots in a row. Another variant in play is that if the object conker is hit and spins in a complete 360° arc (known as the WINDMILL) the hitter is entitled to an additional shot. Depending on local rules, if the two conker laces become entwined during the game then the first player to shout 'STRINGSIES' receives a free hit. Conker scoring is cumulative; a new conker is always a 'one-er' and its score increases by adding the score of its defeated opponents[†]. For example, if a 'one-er' smashes another 'one-er' it becomes a 'two-er'. If a 'six-er' destroys a 'three-er' it becomes a 'nine-er'; and so on. Because of this unique historic

scoring method, and because most conkers tend to be kept from one season to the next, scrupulous honesty in declaring the true score of a conker is a prerequisite of fair play. A host of (often underhand) techniques exists to temper conkers. These range from FREEZING or ROASTING, to soaking in VINEGAR or STORAGE in a warm dark place (the sock-drawer seems to be an ideal location). As a result of these rather dubious techniques most organised conker competitions insist that only 'house conkers' are played. Importantly, if either conker falls to the ground during a game, it may be stamped upon and crushed by an opponent unless 'NO STAMPSIES' is shouted.

† There is a school of thought which claims, somewhat vociferously, that new conkers should start as a 'none-ers'. This unsound and frankly reckless assertion risks making a mockery of the traditional scoring method. For if a conker's score is increased by adding to it the score of each defeated conker, a 'four-er' beating a virgin 'none-er' would remain a 'four-er' when, in fact, simple logic dictates that it should by rights become a 'five-er'.

FRENCH BOXING

La boxe française was a form of fighting, pioneered by Charles Lecour in the 1830s where the use of the feet was both admitted and encouraged.

Charles VIII of France, while walking in a tennis-court with his Queen, hit his head against a low door which caused his death.

Bradley Stone, Jimmy Murray, and Steve Watt are just a few of those who have died as a consequence of boxing injuries. A host of others, most famously Michael Watson and Gerald McClellan, have suffered serious disabilities.

Thomas Grice was killed when, during a game of football in 1897, he stumbled, fell, and punctured his stomach with his belt buckle.

In 1925 the jockey Frank Hayes suffered a heart attack during a race at Belmont Park, New York, and was in fact dead when he and his horse (Sweet Kiss) crossed the finishing line in first place.

Captain Matthew Webb, the first man to swim across the Channel (see p.59), died in the insane attempt to swim the rapids and whirlpools below Niagara Falls. Of Webb's attempt, one writer opined 'his object was not suicide, but money and imperishable fame'.

Frederick Lewis, Prince of Wales, died having been struck on the bonce with a cricket-ball.

Louis VI died when his horse stumbled after a pig ran under it.

William III died after his horse stumbled over a mole-hill.

José Cándido became the first *matador* to be killed in the ring when he was gored to death by the bull 'Coriano' on 23 June 1771 at Puerto de Santa María.

In 1977 Bing Crosby died (albeit of heart failure) while playing a round of golf in Madrid.

After scoring the own-goal that gave the US victory over Colombia in a 1994 World Cup game, Andrés Escobar was gunned down outside a Medellín nightclub. It is said that the 27-year-old was shot six times by gunmen who taunted him by shouting 'Goal! Goal!'.

Rod Hull, the comedian behind (or inside) Emu, died at the age of 63 while watching the televised Champions' League quarter-final between Manchester United and Inter Milan in 1999. Annoyed by poor reception, Hull climbed onto the roof of his West Sussex cottage to adjust the aerial, but slipped and fell to his death.

Mal 'King Kong' Kirk (1936–87) died of a heart attack possibly precipitated by being crushed under the 26-stone girth of pro-wrestler Big Daddy (see p.50).

Ivan IV 'the Terrible' (1530–84) died while playing chess.

It has been claimed that the Prime Minister Palmerston (1784–1865) died while having sex with a parlour-maid on his billiard table.

—— SOME SPORTING DEATHS OF NOTE cont. ——

During the 1982 World Fencing Championships in Rome, Soviet Vladimir Smirnov died when his opponent's foil snapped and pierced Smirnov's mask.

When Australia defeated England at the Oval in 1882, by 7 runs, the *Sporting Times* printed a mocking obituary to English cricket's death:

In Affectionate Remembrance of English Cricket, Which died at the Oval on 29th August, 1882. Deeeply lamented by a large circle of sorrowing friends and acquaintances. R.I.P. N.B. The body will be cremated and the ashes taken to Australia.

Some weeks later, an English team set off to tour Australia, beating them 2–1†. Afterwards a group of Melbourne ladies presented the English with the burnt remains of a bail which was entombed in a small brown urn about 4" high.
† *An Australian win was deemed unofficial.*

A Dutch woman was killed by a football-playing dolphin at a water park in Holland. The dolphin tossed a ball into the crowd as part of its act, but the ball struck the woman on the head, causing her to fall down a flight of stairs.

Presumably a number of sporting deaths were avoided after Italy won the World Cup in 1938. It is said that Mussolini sent the team a telegram before the match which read simply: 'Win or Die'.

Esteban Domeño became the first recorded fatality of the Pamplona Bull Run (see p.20) when he was gored to death in 1924.

In 1984, Jim Fixx, author of the *Complete Book of Running* and its sequel *Jim Fixx's Second Book of Running*, died of a heart attack while out jogging.

Apparently, all 11 members of the Republic of Congo football team *Bena Tshadi* died after being struck by lightning in 1998. Suspicions both of witchcraft and foul play arose when it emerged that the team they had been playing at the time, *Basangana*, all survived.

George Summers was the first man to be killed by a cricket ball while playing in a first-class game. While batting for Notts *vs* MCC in 1870 a delivery by J. Platts pitched off a pebble and struck his temple.

During the 1955 24-hour Le Mans, Pierre Levegh's Mercedes crashed into the crowd killing Levegh and over 80 spectators. As a mark of respect, Mercedes-Benz withdrew from all motor racing, only returning in 1987.

In February 2002, a bridge game held in Oslo to celebrate the 75th birthday of Willy Seljelid turned surreal when all four players were discovered shot dead. Police found a .22 hunting rifle at the scene, but were unable to ascertain which of the four men was the murderer.

FORMULA 1 PIT CREW

[a] fire-extinguisher man · [b] rear jack man · [c] wheel on · [d] gun man · [e] wheel off & starter motor · [f] dead man's handle · [g] exhaust-shield man · [h] hose support · [i] fuel-nozzle man · [j] rig programmer · [k] rad-duct cleaner · [l] wheel off · [m] gun man · [n] wheel on & front wing adjuster · [o] front jack man · [p] lollipop man · [q] wheel on & front wing adjuster · [r] gun man · [s] wheel off · [t] visor cleaner & rad-duct cleaner · [u] car steady · [v] wheel on · [w] gun man · [x] wheel off

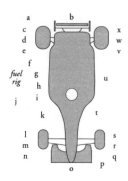

SLOT MACHINES

The US Nevada Gaming Commission defines slot machines as follows:

…any mechanical, electrical or other device, contrivance or machine which, upon insertion of a coin, currency, token or similar object therein, or upon payment of any consideration whatsoever, is available to play or operate, the play or operation of which, whether by reason of the skill of the operator or application of the element of chance, or both, may deliver or entitle the person playing or operating the machine to receive cash, premiums, or merchandise, tokens or anything of value whatsoever, whether the payoff is made automatically from the machine or in any other manner whatsoever.

TEST MATCH SPECIAL NICKNAMES

Johnners	Brian Johnston[†]	*Bachers*	Peter Baxter
Blowers	Henry Blofeld	*The Bearded Wonder*	Bill Frindall
Aggers	Jonathan Agnew[†]	*Bumble*	David Lloyd
CMJ	Christopher Martin-Jenkins	*The Alderman*	Don Mosey
ARL	Tony Lewis	*The Boil*	Trevor Bailey
Balston	Rex Alston	*Foxy*	Graeme Fowler
McFillers	Alan McGillvray	*The Doctor*	Neville Oliver

[†] 'The most professional piece of broadcasting I ever did' is how Johnners described his now legendary on-air laughing hysteria. In 1991 Agnew described how Ian Botham had got out by nudging off a bail while straddling his wicket after an attempted hook. Aggers quipped 'he didn't quite manage to get his leg over' – which reduced Johnners to helpless giggles lasting several minutes, interrupted with the plaintive plea: 'Do stop it, Aggers!'

—— A GLOSSARY OF FOX HUNTING TERMS ——

All on......what the whipper-in says when the hounds are accounted for

Babble...........a hound that *speaks* when there is no scent or no quarry

Biddable...an obedient hound

Blank....................................failing to find a fox in a *covert*

Brush...the fox's tail

Burning..a very strong scent

Burst...the first part of a run

Cap ....fee paid to have a day's hunting

Checking....when hounds stop after a break in the scent or a disruption

Chop ....to kill a sleeping fox

Covert ....a wood, thicket, or copse used as refuge by the fox

Cut a voluntary ....to fall off one's horse while hunting

Doubling the horn.....notes very quickly blown to summon the hounds

Earth ....a fox's underground refuge

Fadge ....a slow pace, somewhere between a walk and a trot

Gone to ground.....................when a fox takes refuge in an *earth*

Holla................vocal call made to notify the huntsman of the quarry

Jink.......................................a sharp turn made by the quarry

Line...........the progress and direction of a hunt as it chases its quarry

Make a pack.......................................count the hounds

Mask..the fox's head or face

MFH ....Master of Fox Hounds

Moving off ....leaving the meet to start a day's hunting

Music ....the sound made by the hounds when running

Mute ....a hound that does not *speak*

Rate[†].......................................to discipline or scold a hound

Riot[†].........when hounds pursue the wrong quarry (deer, rabbits, etc.)

Scarlet[‡]................................the 'correct' name for a red coat

Sinking..an exhausted fox

Speak ....when a hound barks as it hunts the *line*

Stern...a hound's tail

Tantivy...riding at full gallop

Unentered ....a young hound yet to hunt

View ....to sight a fox

Walking out...................................daily exercise of hounds

Whelps ....puppies

Whipper-in ...a hunt employee who works as the MFH's right-hand man

† When hounds *riot* they are *rated* depending on the quarry they are chasing: Deer – 'ware haunch' · Hare or rabbits – 'ware hare' · Birds – 'ware wing' · Cars – 'ware motor'.
‡ Many use the term 'pink' to describe hunting scarlet. This usage seems to derive not from any colour association, but rather from a (possibly fictitious) C19th tailor called Pink (or Pinque) who apparently made the best hunting attire. However, since no records of any famous tailor called Pink have been found, it seems likely that he never existed.

THE MODERN OLYMPICS

Season	Host city	Year	No. of sports	Male athletes	Female athletes	No. of nations	GB golds	GB silvers	GB bronzes	Most golds	N°
S	Athens	1896	9	241	0	14	2	3	2	United States	11
S	Paris	1900	18	975	22	24	15	6	9	France	25
S	St Louis	1904	17	639	6	12	1	1	0	United States	77
S	London	1908	22	1971	37	22	56	51	38	Great Britain	56
S	Stockholm	1912	14	2359	48	28	10	15	16	United States	25
S	Antwerp	1920	22	2561	65	29	16	15	13	United States	41
S	Paris	1924	17	2954	135	44	9	13	12	United States	45
W	Chamonix	1924	6	247	11	16	1	1	2	Norway	4
S	Amsterdam	1928	14	2606	277	46	3	10	7	United States	22
W	St Moritz	1928	4	438	26	25	0	0	1	Norway	6
S	Los Angeles	1932	14	1206	126	37	4	7	5	United States	41
W	Lake Placid	1932	4	231	21	17	0	0	0	United States	6
S	Berlin	1936	19	3632	331	49	4	7	3	Germany	33
W	Garmisch-Partenkirchen	1936	4	566	80	28	1	1	1	Norway	7
S	London	1948	17	3714	390	59	3	14	6	United States	38
W	St Moritz	1948	4	592	77	28	0	0	2	Norway	4
S	Helsinki	1952	17	4436	519	69	1	2	8	United States	40
W	Oslo	1952	4	585	109	30	1	0	0	Norway	7
S	Melbourne	1956	17	2938	376	72	6	7	11	USSR	37
W	Cortina d'Ampezzo	1956	4	687	134	32	0	0	0	USSR	7
S	Rome	1960	17	4727	611	83	2	6	12	USSR	43
W	Squaw Valley	1960	4	521	144	30	0	0	0	USSR	7

THE MODERN OLYMPICS

Season	Host city	Year	No. of sports	Male athletes	Female athletes	No. of nations	GB golds	GB silvers	GB bronzes	Most golds	No.
S	Tokyo	1964	19	4473	678	93	4	12	2	United States	36
W	Innsbruck	1964	6	892	199	36	1	0	0	USSR	11
S	Mexico City	1968	20	4735	781	112	5	5	3	United States	45
W	Grenoble	1968	6	947	211	37	0	0	0	Norway	6
S	Munich	1972	23	6075	1059	121	4	5	9	USSR	50
W	Sapporo	1972	6	801	205	35	0	0	0	USSR	8
S	Montreal	1976	21	4824	1260	92	3	5	5	USSR	49
W	Innsbruck	1976	6	892	231	37	1	0	0	USSR	13
S	Moscow	1980	21	4064	1115	80	5	7	9	USSR	80
W	Lake Placid	1980	6	840	232	37	1	0	0	USSR	10
S	Los Angeles	1984	23	5263	1566	140	5	11	21	United States	83
W	Sarajevo	1984	6	998	274	49	1	0	0	Germany	9
S	Seoul	1988	25	6197	2194	159	5	10	9	USSR	55
W	Calgary	1988	6	1122	301	57	0	0	0	USSR	11
S	Barcelona	1992	28	6652	2704	169	5	3	12	Former-USSR	45
W	Albertville	1992	7	1313	488	64	0	0	0	Germany	10
W	Lillehammer	1994	6	1215	522	67	0	0	2	Russia	11
S	Atlanta	1996	26	6806	3512	197	1	8	6	United States	44
W	Nagano	1998	7	1389	787	72	0	0	1	Germany	12
S	Sydney	2000	28	6582	4069	199	11	10	7	United States	40
W	Salt Lake City	2002	7	1513	886	77	1	0	1	Norway	13
S	Athens	2004	28	tbc	tbc	202	9	9	12	United States	35

———————— SLEEPING & JERKING ————————

HYPNOGOGIC JERKS	HYPNOPOMPIC JERKS
The spasmodic jerks which occur just at the point of falling asleep.	The spasmodic jerks which occur just at the point of waking up.

—— DERBIES, CLASSICS, & GRUDGE MATCHES ——

North Scotland	*curling, the 'Grand Match'* [1]	South Scotland
Commons	*Parliamentary tug of war*	Lords
Real Madrid	*football, 'el classico'*	Barcelona
Rangers	*football, the 'Old Firm'* [2]	Celtic
Gentlemen	*pre-professional cricket*	Players
Labergorce	*polo*	Black Bears
Big Daddy[3]	*1970s & 1980s 'pro' wrestling*	Giant Haystacks
Hibs	*football, the 'Edinburgh derby'*	Hearts
Oxford	*'the' boat race*	Cambridge
Eton	*schoolboy cricket* [4]	Harrow
Kingussie	*shinty*	Newtonmore
Cannock	*field hockey*	Reading
Kasparov	*human vs computer chess* [5]	IBM's Deep Blue
Stockport	*lacrosse*	Cheadle
Bristol	*backgammon*	Birmingham
London	*fencing*	Rest of Britain
Malory London	*men's volleyball*	London Docklands
England	*cricket, 'the Ashes'* [6]	Australia
Air India	*Kabaddi (India)*	Maharashtra Ind.
Jesters	*Eton fives*	Eton Fives Assoc.
Cork	*hurling*	Tipperary

[1] The *Royal Caledonian Curling Club* Grand Match has not been held since 1979 because successive winters have been too mild to produce the 8"-thick ice required on the lochs. [2] Celtic Manager Tommy Burns said in 1997 that 'the Old Firm match is the only match in the world where the managers have to calm the interviewers down'. [3] The real name of both Big Daddy *and* his father was Shirley Crabtree (see also p.102). [4] Eton and Harrow enjoy a longstanding rivalry and each institution, like the Houses of Commons and Lords, occasionally refers to its opposite number as 'the other place' (cf. Uncle Monty in *Withnail & I*). Both schools have blue as their colour: Harrow is dark blue, a colour shared with Oxford; Eton is light blue, a colour shared with Cambridge ever since the first boat race (see p.19) when a consignment of ribbon was used to identify their crew. The first Eton *vs* Harrow match at Lord's was played in 1805 – Lord Byron played for Harrow. [5] Garry Kasparov played the IBM supercomputer Deep Blue for the first time in 1996 and, by switching strategies mid-game, beat the machine 4–2. In a rematch a year later, a modified Deep Blue beat Kasparov 3½–2½. In 1998 Deep Blue became the first computer to achieve the Grandmaster rating. [6] See p.45. [For the longstanding rivalries of Siena's *Palio* see pp.86–7.]

CONTRACT BRIDGE SCORING

TRUMPS				*for each trick over 6 bid & made*	NO TRUMPS	
♣	♦	♠	♥		1st trick	Others
20	20	30	30	Undoubled	40	30
40	40	60	60	Doubled	80	60
80	80	120	120	Redoubled	160	120

The 1st to score 100 points below the line, in 1 or more hands, wins a game

HONOURS	RUBBER BONUS
Scored above the line by either side	Two-game rubber 700
Any 4 AKQJT in a suit bid 100	Three-game rubber 500
All 5 AKQJT in a suit bid 150	Unfinished rubber – 1 game .. 300
All 4 Aces in No Trump bid .. 150	Part Score 100

PREMIUMS – *scored above the line for the Declarer*

Making Doubled contract 50	Making Redoubled contract .. 100

NOT VULNERABLE	*over tricks*	VULNERABLE
Trick value .... Undoubled .... Trick value
100 .... Doubled 200
200 .... Redoubled 400
500 .... Small Slam bonus (bid of 6) 750
1000 .... Grand Slam bonus (bid of 7) 1500

NOT VULNERABLE			*failed contract penalty*			VULNERABLE
Undoubled	Doubled	Redoubled	Undertricks	Undoubled	Doubled	Redoubled
50	100	200	one	100	200	400
100	300	600	two	200	500	1000
150	500	1000	three	300	800	1600
200	800	1600	four	400	1100	2200
250	1100	2200	five	500	1400	2800
300	1400	2800	six	600	1700	3400

SPHAIRISTIKE

Sphairistike is the name by which lawn tennis used to be known. The game was invented by Major Walter Clopton Wingfield, who introduced it in 1873 to a Christmas party in Nantclywd, Wales. The game borrowed heavily from the existing games of Royal Tennis and badminton and was played on an hourglass-shaped court with a net 5' high. The Major named the game *Sphairistike* (Greek for 'ball playing') but affectionately called it *Sticky*. As the game's popularity grew this unpronounceable name was rejected in favour of something less silly, and 'lawn tennis' was born.

──────── THATCHER ON THE IDLE YOUNG ────────

Young people ought not to be idle. It is very bad for them.

— MARGARET THATCHER, *The Times*, 1984

──── MONOPOLY: (UN)DESIRABLE PROPERTIES ────

The cheapest and costliest properties on a selection of Monopoly boards:

cheapest	*board*	*costliest*
Old Kent Road	London	Mayfair
Ronda De Valencia	Spain	Paseo Del Prado
Tire Yard	Springfield	Burns Manor
Badstrasse	Germany	Schlossallee
Tupelo Boyhood Home	Elvis	Graceland
Boulevard De Belleville	France	Rue De La Paix
S.S. Swine Trek	Muppets	Kermit the Frog's Swamp
Dorpsstraat Ons Dorp	Holland	Kalverstraat Amsterdam
Yoda's Hut	Star Wars Classic	Imperial Palace
Chur Kornplatz	Switzerland	Zürich – Paradelplatz
Musgrave Road	South Africa	Eloff Street
Mediterranean Avenue	USA [standard]	Boardwalk
ΟΔΟΣ ΚΥΨΕΛΗΣ	Greece	ΛΕΩΦΟΡΟΣ ΑΜΑΛΙΑΣ
Palace Station	Las Vegas	The Strip
Auntie Em's Farm	Wizard of Oz	Home Sweet Home
South Street Seaport	New York (1994)	Trump Tower
Central Park	New York (1996)	The Plaza
Bronx	New York (1998)	Fifth Avenue
Västerlanggatan	Sweden	Norrmalmstorg
Biker Alley	Batman & Robin	Wayne Manor
Finsensvej	Denmark	Nytorv
Todd Street	Australia	Kings Avenue
Campo Grande	Portugal	Rossio
Crumlin	Ireland	Shrewsbury Road
Cheung Chau	Hong Kong (1997)	The Peak
Chep Lap Kok	Hong Kong (2000)	Victoria Peak
Gypsy's Covered Wagon	Scooby Doo	The Creeper's Bell Tower

──────────── RELAY RACE BATONS ────────────

The specifications of batons suitable for use in Olympic relay race events:
Length 28–30cm · Circumference 12–13cm · Weight >50gm

— GOWERS-ROUND'S RULES OF FRENCH CRICKET —

Polymath sportsman 'Sir' Wilfred Gowers-Round[†] (1845–1955) devised a set of rules for French Cricket, declaring: *'it is a versatile game. It can be played with any number of players, of any age or sex, on almost any ground. However, just because the game is informal (and enjoyable to play), it does not follow that it can be played with insouciant disregard for order, fairness, and good sense.'*

The first batsman is chosen either by mutual consent, or by spinning the bat and calling on which side it lands. The batsman nominates the first bowler, and can place them anywhere he likes in the field. The batsman must stand in the centre of the ground with his feet touching. He may not move his feet during his innings [q.v. PURLEY variant]. The so called 'Flamingo Stance' is strictly prohibited in all play. A batsman may be out in five ways: [i] *Bowled Out* · when the ball touches any part of the foot, ankle, or leg (below the knee), including loose clothing. [ii] *Caught Out* · when a fielder catches the ball directly from the bat, the handle, or the batsman's hand or arm (below the wrist[‡]). [iii] *One Hand One Bounce* · as in [ii] but the ball may bounce once on the ground so long as it is cleanly caught with only one hand. [iv] *Hit Ball Twice.* [v] *Six and Out* · If the ball is hit over an agreed boundary (e.g. a hedge). No batsmen may be given out under any circumstances on the first ball of their innings.

Fielders may stand wherever they choose – as close to the batsman as they dare. Bowlers must bowl the ball from where they have fielded it. Bowlers must bowl under-arm at all times. Half-volleys, balls rolled along the ground ('daisy cutters'), and full-tosses are all permitted. It is permitted to feint a bowl (colloquially known as 'foxing') – however, over-use of the feint is frowned upon in social play. The ball may be bowled as soon as it has been fielded, but bowlers may be disqualified if they are deemed to bowl belligerently.

When a batsman is out, the person responsible for taking the 'wicket' assumes the bat [q.v. ROSS variant].

There is no scoring. The batsman who has enjoyed the longest innings is deemed the victor.

The PURLEY variant allows the batsman to turn his feet, on his spot, so that he faces the bowler, but *only* if he has hit the ball. The SIR DENNIS variant allows fielders to pass the ball between themselves before bowling so as to out-manoeuvre the batsman. (For obvious reasons SIR DENNIS and PURLEY variants are rarely played together.) The ROSS variant allows the order of batsmen to rotate in turn, creating an informal game.

† Sir Wilfred was such a fan that the game was known by some as *'Gowers-Rounders'.*
‡ Introduced in response to the leg theory of the 1932–3 bodyline Tour (see p.121).

WIGHTMAN'S TENNIS ABECEDARIAN

Hazel Wightman (1886–1974) won numerous national and international titles in her long and distinguished career, earning herself the nickname 'the Queen Mother of Tennis'. In 1923 she presented the first Wightman Cup to the winners of the, now annual, US *vs* UK women's tennis match. In her classic 1933 book *Better Tennis*, Wightman presents her 'Letters of Advice' – an alphabet of admonitions for the aspiring tennis champion.

Always Alert **B**e Better **C**oncentrate Constantly **D**on't Dally **E**ver Earnest **F**air Feeling **G**et Going

Hit Hard **I**mitate Instructor **J**ust Jump **K**eep Keen **L**ess Loafing **M**ove Meaningly **N**ever New

Only Over **P**raise Partner **Q**uash Qualms **R**elax Rightly **S**tand Straight **T**ake Time **U**mpire Usually

Vary Volleys **W**ork Wiles **X**ceed Xpectations **Y**ell Yours **Z**ip Zip

SPORT & THE SOCIAL DIVIDE

In the case of almost every sport one can think of, from tennis to billiards, golf to skittles, it was royalty or the aristocracy who originally developed, codified and popularised the sport, after which it was taken up by the lower classes.

— MARK ARCHER, *The Spectator*, 1996

STROPS (BACKWARDS SPORTS)

There are a few sports where participants move predominantly backwards:

Swimming (backstroke) · High-jump (the Fosbury Flop[†])
Tug o' war · Rowing · Abseiling (or rappelling)

A host of other sports exist where moving backwards plays a central part: fencing, ice-hockey, shot-put, gymnastics, diving, and curling (sweepers).

[†] The Fosbury Flop was invented by the American athlete Richard 'Dick' Douglas Fosbury (b.1947) as a revolutionary new approach to the high-jump. Fosbury rejected the traditional forward-facing 'straddle technique' and pioneered a method whereby jumpers arched backwards over the bar. After Fosbury won a gold medal at the 1968 Mexico Olympics his ungainly Flop was swiftly adopted as a standard approach to the high-jump.

———————— THE CRESTA RUN ————————

The Cresta is like a woman, but with this cynical difference:
to love her once is to love her always.
— LORD BRABAZON OF TARA

Situated in the charming village of St Moritz, in Switerland's Engadine Valley, the Cresta Run is a ¾-mile toboggan course which riders descend lying face-down on heavy metal 'skeletons' just inches from the ice. There are two starting positions: 'Top' for the experienced rider and, a little lower down, 'Junction' for the nervous. Speeds can easily reach 80mph and the accomplished rider will find himself 514ft closer to sea-level in under a minute. Little can be done in the way of steering, though riders attach metal rakes to their boots to help influence speed and direction. Since the run is carved anew each season from the Alpine snow, its exact structure and dimensions change from year to year – thus securing the Cresta Run's claim to be one of the last great amateur sports in the world.

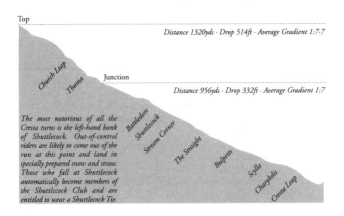

Top

Distance 1320yds · Drop 514ft · Average Gradient 1:7·7

Church Leap

Thoma

Junction

Distance 956yds · Drop 332ft · Average Gradient 1:7

The most notorious of all the Cresta turns is the left-hand bank of Shuttlecock. Out-of-control riders are likely to come out of the run at this point and land in specially prepared snow and straw. Those who fall at Shuttlecock automatically become members of the Shuttlecock Club and are entitled to wear a Shuttlecock Tie.

Battledore
Shuttlecock
Stream Corner
The Straight
Bulpetts
Scylla
Charybdis
Cresta Leap

The Cresta is a powerful and attractive mistress.
She will stand no nonsense when you are learning the ropes, and many
and severe are the rebuffs that she administers to her most ardent suitors.
— SIR JAMES COATS

To date, only four riders have lost their lives on the Cresta Run but, as might be expected, minor and serious injuries are not uncommon. Before novice riders are permitted down the Run, all must attend the infamous 'death talk', at which the dangers of the Cresta are graphically illustrated by a life-size composite of just some of the X-rays riders have required.

STREAKING

The 1970s witnessed an explosion in streaking – an activity defined, rather splendidly, by *The Times* in 1973 as 'racing nude between two unpredictable points'. Although the relationship between human nakedness and sporting endeavour has links back to Greek times, sociologists trace the popularity of streaking amongst spectators to American college campuses which, at times, seemed almost over-run with students in the altogether. (In 1974 the Dean of Memphis State University became so exasperated by naked students he decreed that undergrads caught streaking would be 'suspended'.)

Although streaking has had its knockers, the activity is still popular and few sporting events are safe from the determined exhibitionist: Royal Ascot, Spain's Pamplona bull run, the Tour de France, international synchronised swimming, and even the world snooker championships have all been targeted. Perhaps the most infamous British streakers include Erica Roe (undisputed 'queen of streaking'); Michael O'Brien (pictured left); Michael Angelow; and Mark Roberts who has more than 300 streaks under his non-existent belt, including Wimbledon, the Grand National, and even Crufts.

The campus streaking craze inspired Ray Stevens' novelty record *The Streak*, which was recorded in 1974, spent 3 weeks at No.1 in the USA, and sold over a million copies. In the same year, without doubt the most famous non-sporting streak was performed by 33-year-old Robert Opal, who sauntered naked behind David Niven at the Oscar ceremony. Opinion is divided as to whether or not the exposure of Janet Jackson's nipple by Justin Timberlake during SuperBowl 38's halftime show qualifies as even a very partial streak.

SPECIFIC CARD NICKNAMES

4♣	The devil's four-poster	A♣	The horseshoe; puppy-foot
9♦	The curse of Scotland	4♣	The curse of Mexico
K♥	The suicide King	A♠	Old Frizzle (see p.62)
J♥ & J♠	One-eyed Jacks	K♦	The man with the axe

The etymologies of these nicknames range from the obvious to the obscure. The 'suicide King', for example, is so called because the traditional French picture depicts him about to impale himself on his sword. A similar explanation is behind 'the man with the axe', and the 'one-eyed Jacks'. Considerable debate surrounds the naming of 'the Curse of Scotland', which has been linked to Queen Mary, the Battle of Culloden, the Massacre at Glencoe, Papists, and the design of the St Andrew's Cross. Francis Grose claimed in *The Antiquities of Scotland* (1789) that: 'diamonds ... imply royalty ... and every 9th king of Scotland has been observed for many ages to be a tyrant and a curse to the country'.

———————— STAKHANOV & OBLOMOV ————————

Alexey Grigorievich STAKHANOV (1906–77) was a Soviet coalminer famous in the 1930s for his hardwork and efficiency. (Stakhanov's productivity was over 14 times the norm.) In an attempt to encourage such industrious output Stalin championed 'Stakhanovism' as a model for other Soviet workers. In 1978 Stakhanov's home town of Sergo was renamed in his honour.

Ilya Ilyitch OBLOMOV, created by writer Ivan Goncharov (1812–91), was a man so lazy that he did not rise from his bed for the first 150 pages of his eponymous novel. From this splendid character the notion of 'Oblomovism' developed – a state of languorous inertia, endemic in Russia's intelligentsia, caused by a fundamental idleness common in the Slavonic character.

——TENNIS GRAND-SLAM, SURFACES, & MONTHS——

Australian Open *(Rebound Ace)* [Jan] · French Open *(red clay)* [May/Jun]
Wimbledon *(grass)* [Jun/Jul] · US Open *(cement)* [Aug/Sep]

———————————— THE VOICE OF … ————————————

Some of the voices that have become inexorably associated with a sport:

Murray Walker . . . . . . motor racing
John Arlott . . . . cricket (see also p.46)
Kenneth Wolstenholme[1] . . football
Bill McLaren . . . . rugby union
Ron Pickering . . . . athletics
John Snagge[2] . . . . the boat race
Peter O'Sullevan . . . . racing
Harry Carpenter . . . . boxing
Kent Walton[3] . . . . wrestling
Digby Willoughby . . . . Cresta Run

Dan 'Oh I say!' Maskell . . . . . . tennis
Peter Alliss . . . . golf
Dorian Williams . . . show jumping
Martin Fitzmaurice[4] . . . . darts
Dennis Cometti . . . . . . Aussie rules
'Whispering' Ted Lowe[5] . . snooker
Michael O'Hehir . . . . Gaelic games
John Friend . . . . Henley Regatta
Peter Kneale . . . . . . Isle of Man TT
Eddie Waring . . . . rugby league

[1] Wolstenholme's most famous comment was undoubtedly made on Saturday 30 July 1966 during the England *vs* West Germany World Cup final at Wembley. It was during this game that he intoned the immortal words: 'Some people are on the pitch. They think it's all over … [Geoff Hurst scores his hat-trick to make it 4–2] … it is now!' [2] Snagge was responsible for the glorious statement of the obvious during the 1949 boat race when he declared 'I can't see who's in the lead – but it's either Oxford or Cambridge'. [3] Walton welcomed viewers to ITV's *World of Sport* with a husky 'Greetings, grapple fans!'. [4] A few contenders exist for this title including Sid Waddell and, of course, Jim Bowen's sidekick on the *Bullseye* oche Tony 'Iiiiin One' Green – 'look what you could have won'. [5] Ted Lowe is responsible for one of the most unhelpful commentaries: 'He's going for the pink, and for those of you with black and white sets, the yellow is behind the blue'.

TOUR DE FRANCE JERSEY COLOURS

Jersey colour	Introduced	Awarded for
Yellow	1919	overall fastest time
Green	1953	most points
White & red polka-dot	1975	best climber
White	1975	best young rider (≤25)

The Yellow Jersey is so coloured because the original race sponsor – the newspaper *L'Auto* – was printed on yellow paper. The red and white shirt owes its origin to the sponsor Poulain chocolates; and the green shirt to the gardening shop Belle Jardinier. Between 1984 and 1988 a red jersey was awarded to the leader of the intermediate sprint bonus competition. A Competitiveness Prize is awarded at each stage to the rider who has made the most effort and has demonstrated the best sportsmanship. The Competitiveness Prize winner for each particular stage wears special blue number bibs for the following stage; and the most aggressive and combative rider in each stage wears special red number bibs.

LOTUS-EATERS

The lotus-eaters of Greek myth dwelt on the ever-shifting sandbanks of waters near Carthage. There they ate the fruit of the lotus – not the water-lilies of Egypt, but plants with roots in the underworld that drew water from the river Lethe. This water had the power to remove all memories, and the lotus-eaters (or Lotophagi) lived in an idle, paralysed, trancelike state with neither recollection of the past nor concept of the future, and with no desire to return to their native lands. As Odysseus sailed home from Troy, he landed on one of these sandbanks and sent three men out to explore. The men discovered the Lotophagi, ate of their fruit, and were sucked into a twilight state of idle paralysis before being dragged weeping back to their ship, pleading to be left behind. In his 1833 poem *Song of the Lotos-Eaters*, Alfred Tennyson used this myth to explore our desire to reject the prosaic world of toil for a more languorous state of idleness:

> Let us swear an oath, and keep it with an equal mind,
> In the hollow Lotos-land to live and lie reclined
> On the hills like Gods together, careless of mankind.

RACECOURSE HANDEDNESS OF NOTE

LEFT-HAND	RIGHT-HAND
Aintree · Ayr · Cheltenham	Ascot · Beverley · Exeter
Chepstow · Chester · Doncaster	Goodwood · Huntingdon
Epsom · Haydock · Newbury	Kempton · Newmarket · Ripon
Newcastle · Uttoxeter · York	Salisbury · Sandown · Taunton

── SWIMMING THE ENGLISH CHANNEL ──

The first successful cross-Channel swim was accomplished by Captain Matthew Webb who, heavily greased with porpoise oil, took 21¾ hours to swim from Dover to Calais on 24–5 August 1875. (Only twelve days earlier, Webb had been forced by poor weather to abandon an attempt at the crossing, complaining that there was 'too much sea on'.) Webb swam a slow and stately breast-stroke (20 to the minute), and fortified himself with beef-tea, beer, coffee, cod-liver oil, and – to counteract the effects of a nasty sting by a yellow star-fish – even brandy. Webb's route was thus:

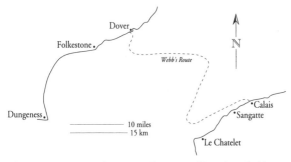

After Webb's crossing, the Mayor of Dover said 'I make so bold to say that I don't believe that in the future history of the world any such feat will be performed by anybody else'. But, while it took 36 years for Webb's feat to be repeated, since then a multitude have made the crossing, employing a range of styles: backstroke, Australian crawl, and the curious Trudgeon stroke (scissor kicks with a double over-arm). Below are a few records:

date	feat (CROSSING DIRECTION)	name	time
1875	*1st solo crossing* (E–F)	M. Webb [UK]	21:45
1911	*2nd solo crossing* (E–F)	T.W. Burgess [UK]	22:35
1923	*1st solo crossing* (F–E)	Enrico Tiraboschi [ITA]	16:33
1926	*1st female solo crossing* (F–E)	Gertrude Ederle [USA]	14:39
1934	*1st to beat Webb's time* (E–F)	E. Temme [UK]	15:34
1951	*1st female solo crossing* (E–F)	Florence Chadwick [USA]	16:19
1961	*1st non-stop return crossing*	Antonio Abertondo [ARG]	43:10
1978	*1st under-16* [13y 233d] (E–F)	Karl Beniston [UK]	12:25
1981	*1st triple crossing* (E–F–E–F)	Jon Erikson [USA]	38:27
1982	*1st crossing by a Chilean* (E–F)	Victor Contraras [CHI]	12:02
1989	*1st butterfly-stroke* (E–F)	Vicki Keith [CAN]	23:33

Glaswegian Jabez Wolffe attempted the Channel crossing 22 times and failed on each occasion. In 1911 a bagpipe player accompanied him by boat to help him set a rhythm – but to no avail. For the curious, tragic, and strangely ironic drowning of Captain Matthew Webb see p.44.

—— THE QUEENSBERRY RULES OF BOXING · 1864 ——

1. To be a fair stand-up boxing match in a twenty-four foot ring or as near to that size as possible.

2. No wrestling or hugging allowed.

3. The rounds to be of 3 minutes' duration and 1 minute time between rounds.

4. If either man falls through weakness or otherwise, he must get up unassisted, 10 seconds to be allowed him to do so, the other man meanwhile to return to his corners, and when the fallen man is on his legs the round to be resumed and continued till the 3 minutes have expired. If one man fails to come to the scratch in the 10 seconds allowed, it shall be in the power of the referee to give his award in favour of the other man.

5. A man hanging on the ropes in a helpless state with his toes off the ground, shall be considered down.

6. No seconds or other person to be allowed in the ring during the rounds.

7. Should the contest be stopped by any unavoidable interference, the referee to name the time and place as soon as possible for finishing the contest, so that the match must be won or lost, unless the backers of the men agree to draw the stakes.

8. The gloves to be fair-sized boxing gloves of the best quality and new.

9. Should a glove burst, or come off, it must be replaced to the referee's satisfaction.

10. A man on his knees is considered down, and if struck is entitled to the stakes.

11. No shoes or boots with springs allowed.

12. The contest in all other respects to be governed by the Revised Rules of the London Prize Ring.

The Marquis of Queensberry was convinced (not unreasonably) that his son Lord Alfred Douglas ('Bosie') was having an affair with Oscar Wilde. On 18 February 1895 the Marquis left a card at the Albermarle Club in London which was addressed: 'To Oscar Wilde posing as a somdomite'. It was this misspelt card that prompted Wilde to bring his disastrous prosecution against Queensberry for libel and defamation. On Wednesday 3 April 1895, the first day of the trial, Wilde testified to a verbal exchange he had with the Marquis: Queensberry – 'If I catch you and my son together in a public restaurant, I will thrash you.' Wilde – 'I do not know what the Queensberry Rules are, but the Oscar Wilde rule is to shoot at sight.' The trial collapsed, and after a second trial, Wilde himself was convicted of indecency, and sentenced to two years in prison with hard labour.

—— GOLDEN FERRETS ——

A GOLDEN FERRET is a golf stroke where the ball is holed from a bunker.

THE NIKE 'SWOOSH'

Alongside McDonald's 'golden arches', Coca-Cola's 'dynamic curve' bottle, the cross, and the crescent, the Nike 'swoosh' is one of the most widely recognised icons on the planet. The swoosh was designed in 1971 by the then graphic design student Carolyn Davidson, who invoiced just $35 for her work. The founder of Nike, Phil Knight, selected the design at the very last minute saying 'I don't love it, but it will grow on me'. 12 years later, by which time the swoosh was known the world over, Davidson was given share options in Nike in recognition of her contribution to one of the most influential brands of all time.

Nike was the Greek winged goddess of victory, of which she is a personification. She was the daughter of the Titan Pallas by Styx (the river of the underworld), and sister of Zelos (rivalry), Kratos (strength), and Bia (force). During the battle between the gods and Titans she sided with the gods, for which she was rewarded by Zeus. Although Nike had few powers, she was considered lucky by the gods with whom she would ride into battle.

PYRRHIC VICTORY, PHOCENSIAN DESPAIR, &c

❦ A PYRRHIC VICTORY is one achieved at such a cost that it is almost indistinguishable from defeat. It seems the term derives from the bellicose antics of Pyrrhus (319–272BC), King of Epirus, who twice beat the Roman army but with casualties so crippling that one commentator wrote 'one more such victory and we are lost'. ❦ A CADMEAN VICTORY is one which immediately places the victor in a disadvantageous position. In Greek myth, Cadmus was the youngest son of Phoenician King Agenor. Cadmus slew a monster which guarded a fresh-water spring and sowed its teeth across the ground like corn. Immediately, an army of soldiers sprang up from the spot where the teeth had fallen and launched an attack. ❦ PHOCENSIAN DESPAIR describes a situation in which victory is snatched unexpectedly from the jaws of defeat. The phrase derives from the men of Phocis who, during Philip II of Macedon's reign (382–336BC), were subject to perpetual attacks from their neighbours for daring to farm the sacred field of Delphi. So great was the Phocensians' despair that they vowed to end their lives in a mass human sacrifice. However, just before mounting the pyre on which their women and children were stacked, the Phocensians mounted a last-ditch attack on their foes and defeated them. ❦ AMYCLAEAN SILENCE describes a reticence to speak that causes defeat. It derives from the inhabitants of Amyclae who were so exasperated by constant rumours of a Spartan attack that they passed a decree forbidding anyone to discuss the subject. When the Spartans actually invaded, the Amyclaens were too scared to mention it and the town was quickly taken. ❦

—————————— CITIUS · ALTIUS · FORTIUS ——————————

Below are Olympic results spanning the C20th. Although many factors must be taken into account (timing accuracy, equipment, &c.) they do suggest that we have indeed got swifter, higher, and stronger (see p.71).

Men's	1900	1920	1960	1980	1992	2000
100 metres	11·0s	10·8s	10·3s	10·2s	9·9s	9·8s
800 metres	2m01s	1m53s	1m46s	1m45s	1m43s	1m45s
Marathon	2h59m	2h32m	2h15m	2h11m	2h13m	2h10m
Long jump	7·185m	7·15m	8·12m	8·54m	8·67m	8·55m
Discus	36·04m	44·68m	59·18m	66·64m	65·12m	69·30m

Women's	1900	1920	1960	1980	1992	2000
100 metres	⁵⁄₄	⁵⁄₄	11·0s	11·0s	10·8s	10·7s
800 metres	⁵⁄₄	⁵⁄₄	2m4s	1m53s	1m55s	1m56s
Long jump	⁵⁄₄	⁵⁄₄	6·37m	7·06m	7·14m	6·99m
Discus (see p.124)	⁵⁄₄	⁵⁄₄	55·10m	69·96m	70·06m	68·40m

—————————— CARD TAX & THE ACE OF SPADES ——————————

Although certain duties on playing cards were exacted by the monarchy in the C17th, only in 1711 was a tax on playing cards first systematically levied. Initially the duty was set at sixpence per pack; it rose to 1 shilling in 1756, 1/6 in 1776, 2 shillings in 1789; and 2/6 in 1801. In an attempt to counter fraud and stem the tide of lost revenue the duty was reduced to 1 shilling in 1828, and in 1862 it fell to threepence – it remained at this rate until the duty was finally abolished in 1960. Over the years a number of methods were employed to show that the duty had been paid. The wrappers could be stamped or embossed, as could the labels used to seal the packs. From 1712 onwards, one of the cards in the pack was additionally marked with a hand stamp. Initially this stamp would have been impressed on any card, but it tended to be the Ace of Spades which was usually at the top of the pack. In 1765 the hand stamping of cards was replaced by the printing of official Aces of Spades by the Stamp Office incorporating the royal coat of arms. In 1828 the Duty Ace of Spades (known colloquially as 'Old Frizzle') was printed by the Stamp Office to indicate that the reduced duty (1 shilling) had been paid. In 1862 the system was changed again. Now, card manufacturers were obliged to use official threepence duty wrappers, but they were free to use whatever design they liked on their Aces of Spades. Most chose to keep the ornate Ace of Spade designs which remain in most packs sold today.

SHOVE HA'PENNY

Constructed from highly polished wood or slate, the shove ha'penny board is usually laid out as in the diagram here, with nine BEDS about 1¼" wide. Players take it in turns to shove five coins from the edge lip of the semi-circular starting block; the eventual aim being (over a series of turns) to place 3 coins in each BED. If a player (or team) gets more than 3 coins into any one BED, the additional coins are scored to the other side. For a coin to score it has to rest entirely within its BED, without touching the separating lines at all. The number of BEDDED coins is totted-up after each 'go' of 5 coins, since part of a player's skill lies in their ability to nudge or tickle coins off the lines and into the beds with other coins. Scores are usually inscribed with chalk onto one or other edge of the board. One version of the game permits any coins that score to be reclaimed and played again at the end of each go, which allows players to make long scoring 'breaks'. Below are some of the traditional shove ha'penny terms and phrases:

Placing 3 coins in a BED in a single go............................ *Sergeant*
Placing all 5 coins into BEDS in a single go .. *Sergeant Major; Gold watch*
Failing to score with any coins in a go .... *Nineteener; Blank*
Playing for BEDS at the end of the board .... *Going upstairs*
A player who fills the BEDS in order........................ *Going in style*
A coin very close to a line .... *Whiskery; Shadey; Tight up; On the mud*
The farthest BED on the board .... *London; Annie's room* (see p.89)
To have one coin in a BED................................. *Lance Jacks up*
To have two coins in a BED.............................. *Corporals about*

PUNTING

Punts are narrow, flat-bottomed boats, ideal for shallow water, used in the past by sportsmen as platforms for fishing or shooting water-fowl. Punts are propelled by leverage using long, narrow punt-poles or 'quants' thrust against the waterbed. Although punting is still enjoyed in many places, including Stratford and on stretches of the Thames, punts are most commonly seen on the Cam in Cambridge and the Cherwell in Oxford. By tradition, Oxford punts have one flat and one rounded end, and their punters stand 'in' the round end at the back. Cambridge punts have two square ends, and their punters stand 'on' the flat platform at the back.

'SWING LOW'

Swing Low, Sweet Chariot is an African American spiritual whose true origin, along with other songs originating under slavery, has been lost in the echo of the oral tradition. However, in 1917 musician Henry Thacker Burleigh (1866–1949) set about preserving some of these spirituals, and it is with his arrangement that most (especially rugby fans) are familiar:

<table>
<tr><td>

Swing low, sweet chariot,
Coming for to carry me home,
Swing low, sweet chariot,
Coming for to carry me home.

</td><td>

If you get there before I do,
Coming for to carry me home,
Tell all my friends I'm coming, too.
Coming for to carry me home.

</td></tr>
<tr><td>

I looked over Jordan, and what did I see?
Coming for to carry me home,
A band of angels coming after me,
Coming for to carry me home.

</td><td>

I'm sometimes up and sometimes down,
Coming for to carry me home,
But still my soul feels heavenly bound,
Coming for to carry me home.

</td></tr>
</table>

FISHING HOOK ANATOMY & SIZE

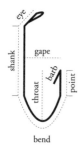

As a rule of thumb, the size of fishing hook needed is proportionate to the fish you hope to ensnare – although this is not always the case. Tench, for example, have mouths softer and smaller than one might expect from their size. A dizzying number of sizing systems have been advanced over the years (Redditch, Kendal, Carlisle, Pennell, to name but a few). However, because fishing hooks have so many variables of size, shape, and angle, a common system of sizing has remained elusive. In general, though, the smaller the hook number, the bigger the hook.

OPERATION

The medical boardgame *Operation* tests the dexterity of players as they perform a variety of surgical tasks for which they earn payment. Below is a list of the 12 operations along with the fees for doctors and specialists:

Doctor's Fee	Operation	Specialist's Fee
500	Bread basket	1000
350	Broken heart	700
250	Butterflies in stomach	500
250	Water on the knee	500
300	Wishbone	600
200	Charlie Horse	400
200	Funny bone	400
150	Writer's cramp	300
150	Adam's apple	300
100	Wrenched ankle	200
100	Spare ribs	200
100	Ankle bone to knee bone	200

THE ORIGINAL HAPPY FAMILIES

family	*trade*	Bung......... brewer	Grits.......... grocer
Block......... barber		Chip ...... carpenter	Pots.......... painter
Bones....... butcher		Dip............. dyer	Soot .... sweep
Bun .... baker		Dose .... doctor	Tape........... tailor

All happy families resemble one another,
each unhappy family is unhappy in its own way.

— LEO TOLSTOY, *Anna Karenina*, 1875–7

BUTTONS

Buttons, like marbles, were a traditional tool of playground games, though the 1859 handbook *Games and Sports for Young Boys* does warn 'we have heard some people say that games with buttons ought not to be countenanced, as they induce boys to cut buttons off their clothes, and transfer them to strings'. (Luckily, the authors dismiss this objection as 'silly and dishonest'.) It seems that children classified their buttons thus:

SINKEYS · metal buttons with a slight hollow in the centre, with holes for the thread to be passed through. A plain SINKEY is a *one-er*; a SINKEY with letters around its edge is a *two-er*.

SHANKEYS · buttons attached by means of a shank or loop of wire. The value of a SHANKEY depends on its size and beauty; if small and plain they are *one-ers*; if more ornamental they are *two-ers*.

LIVERIES · heraldic or lettered buttons worn by livery servants. A small LIVERY counts as a *three-er*; a large LIVERY as a *four-er*, unless it bears a handsome crest, when it is a *six-er*. Bronze buttons, and those ornamented with fox's heads (etc.) are also *six-ers*.

Most games are played with *one-ers* – larger denominations are used as a means of exchanging capital. *Only metal buttons are played with.*

One classic button game is *Pitching at the Line*. A line about 2 foot long is drawn on the ground and, from an agreed distance, the players 'pink' for turns (i.e. the order of play is set by how close these buttons are to the line). The first player then pitches two buttons at the line, aiming so they rest as close to the line as possible without crossing it. The remaining players follow suit. Once all have pitched, the player whose button is nearest to the line claims all the buttons that landed over the line; the remaining buttons he pitches into the air and those that land shank-side uppermost he keeps. All the buttons that remain are divided up equally.

─TRADITIONAL BINGO CALLS─

Kelly's eye............1	Buckle my shoe 32	Baker's bun........61
One little duck......2	Dirty knees........33	Turn the screw....62
You and me.........3	Ask for more.......34	Tickle me...........63
Knock at the door...4	Jump & jive.......35	Red raw 64
Man alive...........5	Three dozen 36	Old-age pension ...65
Tom's tricks.........6	More than eleven ..37	Clickety click 66
Lucky...............7	Christmas cake.....38	Made in heaven ...67
Garden gate.........8	Steps...............39	Saving grace.......68
Doctor's orders 9	Naughty...........40	Either way up 69
Tony's (PM's) den ..10	Life's begun 41	Blind...............70
Legs 11	Winnie the Pooh...42	Bang the drum ...71
One dozen.........12	Down on your knees	Six dozen..........72
Unlucky for some ..13	43	Queen bee.........73
Valentine's day....14	All the fours 44	Candy store........74
Young and keen....15	Halfway there......45	Strive & strive.....75
Sweet..............16	Up to tricks........46	Trombones.........76
Dancing queen 17	Four and seven 47	Sunset strip 77
Coming of age.....18	Four dozen 48	Heaven's gate 78
Goodbye teens......19	PC 49	One more time.....79
One score..........20	Half a century.....50	Eight & blank.....80
Key of the door.....21	Tweak of the thumb	Stop & run........81
Two little ducks....22	51	Straight on through
Thee and me 23	Danny La Rue.....52	82
Two dozen.........24	Stuck in the tree ...53	Time for tea 83
Duck and dive.....25	Clean the floor.....54	Seven dozen 84
Pick and mix......26	Snakes alive........55	Staying alive.......85
Stairs to heaven....27	Was she worth it?..56	Between the sticks..86
Over-weight 28	Heinz varieties.....57	Torquay in Devon .87
Rise and shine 29	Make them wait...58	Two fat ladies......88
Dirty Gertie 30	Brighton line 59	Nearly there 89
Get up and run....31	Five dozen.........60	Top of the shop.....90

─CANASTA SCORING─

4s, 5s, 6s, 7s, 8s, 9s..............5	Impure Canasta................300
10s, Js, Qs, Ks 10	Going out.....................100
2s, Aces 20	Going out concealed..........200
Jokers 50	MINIMUM MELD VALUE TO GO DOWN
Black 3s [where allowed] 5	Negative score..................15
Red 3s 100	Score of 0–1495 50
All 4 Red 3s 800	Score of 1500–2995 90
Pure Canasta.................500	Score of >3000 120

—————— ON WINNING AND LOSING ——————

KNUTE ROCKNE · *Norwegian-born American football coach* · Show me a good and gracious loser, and I'll show you a failure.

IAN FLEMING · The gain to the winner is, in some odd way, always less than the loss to the loser.

TOMMY HITCHCOCK · *US polo player and aviator* · Lose as if you like it; win as if you were used to it.

HENRY 'RED' SANDERS · *American football coach* · Sure, winning isn't everything. It's the only thing.

ERNEST HEMINGWAY · You make your own luck ... You know what makes a good loser? Practice.

VINCE LOMBARDI · Show me a good loser and I'll show you a loser.

MACBETH: If we should fail?
LADY MACBETH: We fail!
But screw your courage to the sticking place, And we'll not fail. [*Macbeth*, I.vii.]

ANONYMOUS · Quitters never win. Winners never quit.

RICHARD NIXON · *writing to Senator Edward Kennedy after the Chappaquiddick debacle in 1969* · A man's not finished when he's defeated; he's finished when he quits.

MARIO PUZO · Show me a gambler and I'll show you a loser; show me a hero and I'll show you a corpse.

CHRIS EVERT · In tennis, at the end of the day you're a winner or a loser. You know exactly where you stand ... I don't need that anymore. I don't need my happiness, my well-being, to be based on winning and losing.

GALEAZZO CIANO · Victory has a hundred fathers but defeat is an orphan. *(This phrase was quoted by President John F. Kennedy after the 1961 Bay of Pigs disaster.)*

MARTINA NAVRATILOVA · The moment of victory is much too short to live for that and nothing else.

MAX BEERBOHM · There is much to be said for failure. It is more interesting than success.

PETER MANDELSON · I am a fighter, not a quitter.

LOUIS KRONENBERGER · The technique of winning is so shoddy, the terms of winning are so ignoble, the tenure of winning is so brief; and the spectre of the has-been – a shameful rather than a pitiable sight these days – brings a sudden chill even to our sunlit moments.

SENECA · Success is not greedy, as people think, but insignificant. That's why it satisfies nobody.

JEAN-PAUL SARTRE · If a victory is told in detail, one can no longer distinguish it from a defeat.

ROLLER-SKATES & MIRRORS

It is claimed that the Belgian Joseph Merlin first invented roller-skates in 1760. Apparently, Merlin wore his skates to a masquerade ball held at Carlisle House in Soho Square, London – but was so unstable on them that he destroyed a mirror worth over £500, and badly wounded himself.

ELEPHANT POLO

It should come as no surprise that a sport as idiosyncratic as elephant polo should have been dreamt up in a St Moritz bar by two dedicated riders of the Cresta Run (see p.55). The brainchild of Jim Edwards, and Olympic tobogganer James Manclark, elephant polo is governed by the World Elephant Polo Association (WEPA), which hosts its annual tournaments on a grass airstrip just outside the Royal Chitwan National Park, in Nepal. Although many similarities exist between elephant polo and its equestrian forerunner, a number of modifications have been made to allow for the inherent differences between horses and pachyderms:

The elephant polo pitch is 120m × 70m (¾ that of a traditional pitch), with 4 players on each side.

Although the game used to be played with footballs, the elephants quickly developed a passion for stamping on the balls until they exploded. Nowadays standard polo balls are used.

Each elephant has two people on its back: the player who strikes the ball, and the *mahout* who handles and steers the elephant.

A game is comprised of two 10-minute chukkas, with a 15-minute interval during which elephants and ends are changed.

To avoid instinctive but dangerous herding behaviour, no team may have more than 3 elephants in one half at any time.

A foul is committed if an elephant lies down in front of the goal-mouth. Similarly, a foul is committed if an elephant picks up the ball with its trunk.

Sticks range from 6–9ft in length, varying on the size of the elephant, and have a traditional mallet head.

Smaller, more nimble elephants are favoured for offensive roles, though older female elephants are often placed defensively near goal to intimidate male competition.

To ensure that the elephants do not overheat, games are not played after midday.

'Ball-boys' are responsible for removing piles of dung, to avoid the possibility of balls becoming ensnared, or excrement being flung by swinging mallets.

SOME SPIN-BOWLING TERMS

OFF-BREAK†	LEG-BREAK	GOOGLY‡

The ball is spun using the fingers to turn the ball in towards a right-handed batsman.	The ball is spun using the wrist to turn the ball away from a right-handed batsman.	The ball comes out of the back of the hand to turn back into the right-handed batsman.

TOP-SPINNER	FLIPPER	LEFT ARM
The leg-spinner changes the position of his wrist so that the ball bounces straight and high.	A low, skidding ball 'squeezed' out between fingers and thumb by leg-spinners.	Orthodox left-handed spinners spin the ball away from right-handed batsmen.

† The DOOSRA is Sri Lankan Muttiah Muralitharan's unorthodox delivery, which turns away from right-handed batsmen. ‡ Also known as the WRONG 'UN or BOSIE (after B.J.T. Bosanquet). The CHINAMAN is the left-arm bowler's version of the GOOGLY. · Arthur Conan Doyle introduced SPEDEGUE'S DROPPER (in a fictional story of the same name) – a ball lobbed 50' into the air that dropped vertically on the stumps, perfected by a schoolmaster who was drafted into the England team and ensured they kept the Ashes.

MARTIAL ART MEANINGS

Martial art	*translation*
AIDO	attacking from the scabbard
AIKIDO	the way of harmony
BAGUAZHANG	eight shapes palms
BUDO	the warrior path
BUGEI	the warrior arts
HAPKIDO	way of coordinated power
JEET KUNE DO	way of the intercepting fist
JUDO	the gentle way
JUJITSU	the gentle technique
KARATE	the way of the empty hand
KENDO	the way of the sword
KENPO	way of the fist
KUNG FU	one who is highly skilled
NINJUTSU	art of invisibility
TAEKWANDO	way of the hands and feet
TAI CHI	great supreme absolute

SYNCHRONISED SWIMMING: DOLPHOLINA

Dolpholina is just one of FINA's elegant synchronised swimming moves:

*Synchronised swimmers may look like cupcakes;
but they're tough cookies.*
— DEMMIE STATHOPLOS

THE SHILL AND THE PROP

In US casino terminology a SHILL is a player (paid an hourly wage by the House) who uses the House's money to drum up business by playing at slow tables. Any money made by the SHILL is returned to the House. In contrast, PROPOSITION PLAYERS or PROPS play with their own money (while receiving a small wage), keeping any profits but shouldering their losses. Both SHILLS and PROPS work under the direction of the House staff, who will move them as required from game to game. In many casinos strict rules exist governing how SHILLS and PROPS may play each game, and requiring the House to identify the paid players if so requested.

—— THE OLYMPIC CREED, MOTTO, & OATHS ——

Although usually attributed to Pierre de Coubertin (1863–1937), the first President of the International Olympic Committee, it seems that the Olympic creed was inspired by a sermon given in St Paul's Cathedral by Ethelbert Talbot, the Bishop of Central Pennsylvania, on 19 July 1908.

The most important thing in the Olympic Games is not to win but to take part, just as the most important thing in life is not the triumph but the struggle. The essential thing is not to have conquered but to have fought well.

De Coubertin is also responsible for instituting the Olympic motto:

CITIUS · ALTIUS · FORTIUS   *swifter · higher · stronger*   (see p.62)

This time de Coubertin borrowed from the French Dominican preacher Father Henri Didon (1840–1900), over whose door the motto was carved. The Olympic Oath, instituted in 1920 and updated in 2000 to address the issue of doping, is taken on behalf of all athletes by a member of the host team. Holding a corner of their national flag, the athlete declaims from the rostrum, in front of the assembled flag-bearers of other nations:

In the name of all the competitors, I promise that we shall take part in these Olympic Games, respecting and abiding by the rules which govern them, committing ourselves to a sport without doping and without drugs, in the true spirit of sportsmanship, for the glory of sport and the honour of our teams.

Since 1972, an officials' oath has also been read by a host-country official:

In the name of all the judges and officials, I promise that we shall officiate in these Olympic Games with complete impartiality, respecting and abiding by the rules which govern them, in the true spirit of sportsmanship.

—— WIMBLEDON RAIN-WARNING CODES ——

A numerical system is employed at Wimbledon to alert and instruct those in charge of covering courts when rain or inclement weather is expected:

1	be on standby, by the court, as there is a concern that it may rain
2	cover the court
3	inflate covers
4	deflate covers (when rain has stopped)
5	uncover court
6	dress the courts for play

— SCRABBLE LETTERS AROUND THE WORLD —

Tile	Turkish value .. no	French value .. no	German value .. no	English value .. no	Spanish value .. no
A	1.... 12	1.... 9	1.... 5	1.... 9	1.... 11
Ä	N/A.... N/A	N/A.... N/A	6.... 1	N/A.... N/A	N/A.... N/A
B	3.... 2	3.... 2	3.... 2	3.... 2	3.... 3
C	4.... 2	3.... 2	4.... 2	3.... 2	2.... 4
Ç	4.... 2	N/A.... N/A	N/A.... N/A	N/A.... N/A	N/A.... N/A
D	3.... 2	2.... 3	1.... 4	2.... 4	2.... 4
E	1.... 8	1.... 15	1.... 15	1.... 12	1.... 11
F	7.... 1	4.... 2	4.... 2	4.... 2	4.... 2
G	5.... 1	2.... 2	2.... 3	2.... 3	2.... 2
Ğ	8.... 1	N/A.... N/A	N/A.... N/A	N/A.... N/A	N/A.... N/A
H	5.... 1	4.... 2	2.... 4	4.... 2	4.... 2
I	2.... 4	1.... 8	1.... 6	1.... 9	1.... 6
İ	1.... 7	N/A.... N/A	N/A.... N/A	N/A.... N/A	N/A.... N/A
J	10.... 1	8.... 1	6.... 1	8.... 1	6.... 2
K	1.... 7	10.... 1	4.... 2	5.... 1	8.... 1
L	1.... 7	1.... 5	2.... 3	1.... 4	1.... 4
LL	N/A.... N/A	N/A.... N/A	N/A.... N/A	N/A.... N/A	8.... 1
M	2.... 4	2.... 3	3.... 4	3.... 2	3.... 3
N	1.... 5	1.... 6	1.... 9	1.... 6	1.... 5
Ñ	N/A.... N/A	N/A.... N/A	N/A.... N/A	N/A.... N/A	8.... 1
O	2.... 3	1.... 6	2.... 3	1.... 8	1.... 8
Ö	7.... 1	N/A.... N/A	8.... 1	N/A.... N/A	N/A.... N/A
P	5.... 1	3.... 2	4.... 1	3.... 2	3.... 2
Q	N/A.... N/A	8.... 1	10.... 1	10.... 1	8.... 1
R	1.... 6	1.... 6	1.... 6	1.... 6	1.... 4
RR	N/A.... N/A	N/A.... N/A	N/A.... N/A	N/A.... N/A	8.... 1
S	2.... 3	1.... 6	1.... 7	1.... 4	1.... 7
Ş	4.... 2	N/A.... N/A	N/A.... N/A	N/A.... N/A	N/A.... N/A
T	1.... 5	1.... 6	1.... 6	1.... 6	1.... 4
U	2.... 3	1.... 6	1.... 6	1.... 4	1.... 6
Ü	3.... 2	N/A.... N/A	6.... 1	N/A.... N/A	N/A.... N/A
V	7.... 1	4.... 2	6.... 1	4.... 2	4.... 2
W	N/A.... N/A	10.... 1	3.... 1	4.... 2	8.... 1
X	N/A.... N/A	10.... 1	8.... 1	8.... 1	8.... 1
Y	3.... 2	10.... 1	10.... 1	4.... 2	4.... 2
Z	4.... 2	10.... 1	3.... 1	10.... 1	10.... 1
Blank	0.... 2	0.... 2	0.... 2	0.... 2	0.... 2
Total	N/A.. 100	N/A.. 102	N/A.. 102	N/A.. 100	N/A.. 100

Scrabble is available in a range of other languages, including: Hebrew, Greek, Arabic, Russian, Bulgarian, Catalan, Czech, Slovak, and Braille.

—HORSE RACING TRACK 'GOING' CONDITIONS—

heavy · soft · good-to-soft · good · good-to-firm · firm · hard
(all-weather course goings: *fast · standard · slow*)

—COMPULSIVE GAMBLING—

Below are a series of questions, devised by the support group *Gamblers Anonymous*, used to help gamblers come to terms with their addiction. Most compulsive gamblers answer yes to at least seven of these questions:

Do you lose time from work due to gambling?
Is gambling making your home life unhappy?
Is gambling affecting your reputation?
Have you ever felt remorse after gambling?
Do you ever gamble to get money with which to pay debts or to
otherwise solve financial difficulties?
Does gambling cause a decrease in your ambition or efficiency?
After losing, do you feel you must return as soon as possible
and win back your losses?
After a win do you have a strong urge to return and win more?
Do you often gamble until your last pound is gone?
Do you ever borrow to finance your gambling?
Have you ever sold anything to finance gambling?
Are you reluctant to use gambling money for normal expenditures?
Does gambling make you careless of the welfare of your family?
Do you gamble longer than you planned?
Do you ever gamble to escape worry or trouble?
Have you ever committed, or considered committing,
an illegal act to finance gambling?
Does gambling cause you to have difficulty in sleeping?
Do arguments, disappointments, or frustrations
create an urge within you to gamble?
Do you have an urge to celebrate any good fortune
by a few hours' gambling?
Have you ever considered self-destruction as a result of your gambling?

—W.G. GRACE AND SPORTSMANSHIP—

The cricketer W.G. Grace is famed almost equally for his questionable sportsmanship as for his skill. Once, having been clean bowled, he turned round, picked up and replaced the bails, and declared to the outraged bowler – 'People have come to see me bat, not to see you bowl!'

—— ARCHAIC GOLF CLUB NOMENCLATURE ——

Few formal links exist between modern and ancient golf clubs, but the list below gives an approximate guide to what comparisons can be made:

Woods No.1	Play Club, Driver		No.4		Jigger, Mashie Iron
No.2	Brassie		No.5		Mashie
No.3	Spoon		No.6		Spade Mashie
No.4	Baffy		No.7		Mashie-Niblick
			No.8		Pitching Mashie
Irons No.1	Driving Iron, Cleek		No.9		Niblick, Baffing Spoon
No.2	Cleek, Midiron		PW/SW		Wedge or Jigger
No.3	Mid-Mashie		Putter/Blank		Putter

The Brassie (or Brassy) was a wooden club with a head shod with brass. The Spoon had a slightly concave head that was handy for playing lofted shots to escape hollows. The Baffy was similarly employed for loft, being described as a short, stiff club with a 'laid back' face. Cleeks (or Cleques) were long-shafted narrow-faced clubs used for distance. The Mashie was a standard club used for medium distance and loft – probably deriving its name from an ancient term for a war-hammer. The Niblick was originally a wooden club, later manufactured as a lofted iron with a short face. It has been suggested that the word Niblick might be a corruption of the Scottish term for a broken nose – *neb laigh*. During the 1971 Apollo 14 mission, Alan Shepard fitted an 8-iron head (equivalent to a pitching mashie) to a 'lunar sample collection device' and hit two golf balls on the Moon. Since 1939, the maximum number of clubs a player is permitted in their bag is 14. This rule cost Ian Woosnam a two-shot penalty when his caddie Miles Byrne left a 15th club – a test driver – in Woosnam's bag during the 2001 Open at Royal Lytham & St Anne's.

———— SOME FLY-FISHING LURES OF NOTE ————

The best fly-fishermen like nothing better than to fashion their own lures to entrap fish. Some of the more elaborate traditional lures are below:

The butcher... *red tail feather, black cock hackle†, crow quill feather wings*
Black Zulu* .... *black ostrich & silver tinsel body, black cock hackle*
Welsh partridge............ *claret seal's fur body, dark partridge feather tail*
Silver blue... *silver tinsel body, blue peacock hackle, dyed-blue feather wings*
Sweep.. *black henny cock hackle, black wings, blue kingfisher feather cheeks*
Coalman.......... *black wool body, teal feather wings, golden pheasant tail*
Pot scrubber .... *copper pot scrubber body, grey squirrel fur wings*
Orange peril .. *orange & green marabou tail, gold tinsel body, orange wings*
Dogstail ...... *beige dog hair tied with brown silk body, reddish cock hackle*
Snipe & purple...... *purple silk body, black hackle from a jack snipe's wing*

†Hackles (or palmers) are made from long neck feathers and are used to alter buoyancy.
*Black Zulu lures were at one time prohibited from competitive angling as too efficient.

—— SOME F1 CIRCUITS OF NOTE ——

Albert Park, Melbourne
Australia [lap:5·303km]

Monte Carlo, Monaco
[lap:3·340km]

Interlagos, Brazil
[lap:4·309km]

Monza, Italy
[lap:5·793km]

Imola, San Marino
[lap:4·933km]

Manama, Bahrain
[lap:5·417km]

Gilles Villeneuve
Canada [lap:4·361km]

Suzuka, Japan [lap:5·807km]

Nürburgring, Germany
[lap:5·148km]

Indianapolis, USA
[lap:4·192km]

Barcelona, Spain [lap:4·730km]

Silverstone, Great Britain
[lap:5·141km]

Hungaroring, Hungary
[lap:4·381km]

Nevers, Magny Cours, France
[lap:4·411km]

Shanghai International, China
[lap:5·451km]

Sepang, Kuala Lumpur
Malaysia [lap:5·543km]

Spa-Francorchamps, Belgium
[lap:6·973km]

Hockenheim, Germany
[lap:4·574km]

CRICKET WICKET SPECIFICATIONS

year	stumps	bails	height	width
1700	2	1	12"	24"
1775	3	1	22"	6"
1798	3	1	24"	7"
1816	3	1	26"	7"
1817	3	2	27"	8"
TODAY	3	2	28"	9"

[In the 1837 *Gentlemen* vs *Players* match *Players* defended wickets 36" high by 12"wide.]

SCHEMATICS OF CROQUET HOOP ORDER

NINE HOOP LAYOUT   SIX HOOP LAYOUT

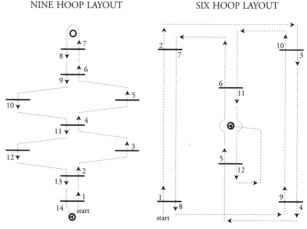

BOLÉRO

Originally of Moroccan origin, the *boléro* was introduced to Spain by Sebastian Zerezo in *c.*1780, and it was quickly adopted as the Spanish national dance. The *boléro* is in 2-4 or 3-4 time resembling the fandango. Maurice Ravel's one-act ballet crescendo *Boléro* (1928) is certainly the most famous example of the dance – in part because it was used in the film *10* where Dudley Moore falls in lust with Bo Derek, but certainly because it was interpreted by Jayne Torvill and Christopher Dean when they won Gold in the 1984 Winter Olympics ice dance. The pair scored 3 × 6·0 and 6 × 5·9 for *technical skill*, and 9 × 6·0 for *artistic impression*.

—— FRAUDS' INTERPRETATION OF DREAMS ——

Oneiromancy – divination by the interpretation of dreams – has long preoccupied mankind. Below are some oneiromantic interpretations from a variety of (frankly dubious) Victorian and Edwardian 'dream guides':

Subject of dream   *denotes*

Alphabet	success through one's own efforts
Ants	one's industry will be rewarded
Bagpipes; bagpipe music	sadness; loss of a loved one
Beavers	danger from hidden enemies
Candles	[lit] pleasing correspondence awaits; [unlit] sickness
Chimney sweeps	excellent fortune ahead
Coffin with flowers	a sick friend will recover
Dancing	good news will come from a long-absent friend
Drowning	financial difficulties await
Earwigs	the risk of persecution or prosecution
Elephants	good fortune; wisdom; new friendships
Finding objects	anxiety about losing something
Frogs	one should be suspicious of strangers or foreigners
Gallows	excellent luck and financial prosperity
Gloves	honour and safety; [torn] disrupted friendship
Hail	grief and sorrow; troubles to be overcome with perseverance
Horseshoes	good luck; a happy home
Ice	great responsibility; plentiful harvest
Jury	disappointment; the need for assistance
Keys	[found] riches and wealth; [lost] disappointment
Kites	a quarrel with friends or relations; uncertainty
Labyrinths	distress; confusion; troubles caused by money or relatives
Lawyers	distress and anguish
Midwives	the revealing of hitherto well-kept secrets
Nails	work, industry, labour; moderate fortune and success
Oranges	misfortune; loss of goods and reputation
Ostriches	trouble through the envy of others
Packages	imminent receipt of a gift or present; fear of change
Peaches	good fortune; success in friendship, business, and love
Queen	imminent good news; fortune in love and romance
Railway	news or a visit from a long-absent friend
Shadow	cares and troubles; [your own] loss, poverty, old age
Squirrels	a prosperous marriage or business alliance; contentment
Tea-pot	new friendship
Urn	[empty] death; [broken] disputes; [with ashes] inheritance
Volcano	bad news; change and uncertainty; family disputes
Wine	happiness; good fortune; festivities
Zebra	the spite of previously trusted friends

GEORGE ORWELL ON THE LOTTERY

The Lottery, with its weekly pay-out of enormous prizes, was the one public event to which the proles paid serious attention. It was probable that there were some millions of proles for whom the Lottery was the principal if not the only reason for remaining alive. It was their delight, their folly, their anodyne, their intellectual stimulant. Where the Lottery was concerned, even people who could barely read and write seemed capable of intricate calculations and staggering feats of memory.

— GEORGE ORWELL, *Nineteen Eighty-Four*, 1949

SOME QUOTATIONS ON CARDS

ELY CULBERTSON · A deck of cards [is] built like the purest of hierarchies, with every card a master to those below it, a lackey to those above it.

ALEXANDER POPE · See how the world its veterans rewards! A youth of frolics, an old age of cards.

SAMUEL JOHNSON · I am sorry I have not learned to play at cards. It is very useful in life: it generates kindness and consolidates society.

CHARLES LAMB · But cards are war, in disguise of a sport.

EDMOND HOYLE · When in doubt, win the trick.

FINLEY PETER DUNNE · Trust everybody, but cut the cards.

F. SCOTT FITZGERALD · A great social success is a pretty girl who plays her cards as carefully as if she were plain.

ARTHUR SCHOPENHAUER · Because people have no thoughts to deal in, they deal cards, and try and win one another's money. Idiots!

ELY CULBERTSON · The bizarre world of cards [is] a world of pure power politics where rewards and punishments [are] meted out immediately. (See also James Bond and Hugo Drax on p.18.)

THE QUALITIES OF A GOOD GREYHOUND

A greyhound should be *heeded* lyke a SNAKE,
And *necked* lyke a DRAKE, *Backed* lyke a BREAM,
Footed lyke a CATTE, *Taylled* lyke a RATTE.

— JULIANA BERNERS, *Book of St Albans*, 1486

─────────── AGAINST FOOTBALL ───────────

A devilishe pastime … and hereof groweth envy, rancour, and malice, and sometimes brawling, murder, homicide, and great effusion of blood.

— PHILIP STUBBES, *Anatomie of Abuses*, 1583

─────── THE FIRST NEWSPAPER CROSSWORD ───────

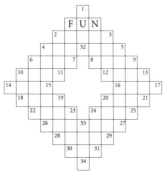

It is thought that the first ever published crossword was this one devised in 1913 by Liverpudlian Arthur Wynne for the American Sunday newspaper the *New York World.* After initial doubts and some experimentation with the diamond shape, the now-familiar square crossword became firmly established. In 1924 the *Sunday Express* printed the UK's first newspaper crossword, and in 1930, *The Times* followed suit.

2–3.... *What bargain hunters enjoy*
6–22........ *What we all should be*
4–5..... *A written acknowledgment*
4–26 .... *A day dream*
6–7 .... *Such and nothing more*
2–11....................... *A talon*
10–11 .... *A bird*
19–28 .... *A pigeon*
14–15 .... *Opposed to less*
F–7 .... *Part of your head*
18–19.......... *What this puzzle is*
23–30.......... *A river in Russia*
22–23........... *An animal of prey*
1–32 .... *To govern*
26–27 .... *The close of a day*
33–34 .... *An aromatic plant*

28–29 .... *To elude*
N–8.......................... *A fist*
30–31 .... *The plural of is*
24–31 .... *To agree with*
8–9................... *To cultivate*
3–12................. *Part of a ship*
12–13....... *A bar of wood or iron*
20–29......................... *One*
16–17 ..... *What artists learn to do*
5–27................... *Exchanging*
20–21 .... *Fastened*
9–25............... *To sink in mud*
24–25 ...... *Found on the seashore*
13–21 .... *A boy*
10–18 *The fibre of the gomuti palm*
[The solution can be found on p.160.]

─────────────── IDLE MONEY ───────────────

Economists term uninvested funds or inactive bank deposits 'idle money'.

CHESS NOTATION

Although a number of different systems of chess notations exist, perhaps the most useful is the Algebraic System. Here, pieces are indicated by these prefixed letters:

K = king · Q = queen · R = rook
B = bishop · N = knight

(pawns are identified by having no prefix)

The eight Ranks and Files are identified with numbers and letters *(as in the diagram opposite)*.

Consequently, each square has a unique designator, from **a8** in the top left-hand corner, to **h1** in the bottom right. The moves made by pieces are indicated by the prefixed letter followed by the square of *arrival* (when pawns are moved, only the square of arrival is noted). If a piece captures another, the letter x is inserted before the square of arrival, for example: Rxd1. When a pawn captures a piece, the file of departure is added before the x and the square of arrival, for example: gxf3. If a pawn is promoted, the move is indicated as normal but the prefix letter of its new identity is added, for example: f8Q. (Other conventions exist for such circumstances as when two identical pieces can move to the same square, and so on.) In addition, a range of other abbreviations are used to describe play, such as:

+	check	?	bad move
++	checkmate	??	serious mistake
0-0	Kingside castling	(?)	questionable move
0-0-0	Queenside castling	!?	interesting, risky move
e.p.	captures *en passant*	?!	dubious, very risky move
1-0	Black resigns (White wins)	!	good move
0-1	White resigns (Black wins)	!!	brilliant move
½-½ or =	draw agreed	⊙	zugzwang

'PULLING THE GOOSE'

In C17th New York, 'Pulling the Goose' was a regular Shrove Tuesday tradition. A live goose was procured, its neck was generously lubricated with soap, oil, or other unguents, and it was tied with rope between two stakes. Contestants on horseback then took it in turn to gallop at full pelt towards the goose, attempting to rip off the bird's head as they passed.

DWYLE FLUNKING

Dwyle Flunking is thought to have originated in the C8th at the court of King Offa of Mercia, probably descending from Spile Troshing (see p.135). Required for the 'sport' are: a bucket of ale; an accordion; a selection of agricultural attire (farmers' jerkins, straw hats, etc.); a rag drenched in ale (the *dwyle*); and a stick to fling the *dwyle* (the *swadger*). Two teams of 12 contest the game, one bats while the other fields. The batsmen take their positions with the *swadger*, while the fielding team links hands in circle around him and dance in an easterly direction to the accompaniment of the accordion player. When the music stops, the batsman flings his *dwyle* at the fielders, scoring 3 runs for a face hit, 2 for torso hit, and 1 for limb hit. They that have the most points after two innings are the winners. The Flemish artist Pieter Bruegel the Elder (*c*.1525–69) appears to depict an unusual variation of Dwyle Flunking in his painting 'Young Folk at Play'.

ACTIVITY AT ALTITUDE

Activity	*metres ± sea-level*
Highest recorded skydive (in pressurised suit)	31,334
Highest point reached by balloonist in pressurised capsule	19,811
Human blood boils	*c*.19,000
Highest a human can go breathing pure oxygen	*c*.12,000
Peak of Everest, highest point on earth	8,850
Mt Aucanquilcha Mine, highest permanent human settlement	5,340
Hernando Siles Stadium, La Paz, Bolivia	3,600
Azteca Stadium, Mexico City	2,240
The Silverlands, Buxton FC ground, Derbyshire	304·8
World record pole vault	6·14
World's lowest golf course, Furnace Creek, Death Valley, USA	-65
Depths reached by freedivers	*c*.-72
Reached by freedivers using weights	-160
Deepest scuba dive	*c*.-313
Depth humans can reach with special equipment	-450
Depth reached by diving elephant seals	-1,500
Krubera Cave, Georgia, deepest cave explored by pot-holers	-1,710
Challenger Deep, Marianas Trench, deepest point in the world	-10,915

On 15 April 1875, H.T. Sivel, Gaston Tissandier, and J.E Croce-Spinelli took off from outside Paris in the balloon *Zenith* to study the effects of altitude. When the balloon reached 8,000m all three were overcome with hypoxia and fainted before they could use the onboard supply of oxygen. As they flickered in and out of consciousness, the three aviators became increasingly confused and mistakenly let fall more ballast, causing them to rise even higher. Tissandier finally woke when the balloon descended to 6,000m, by which time both his companions were dead.

CLASSIC POKER-HAND NICKNAMES

| The AK47 Machine Gun | Magnum *(Colt .44)* | Motown *('Jacks-on-fives')* | The Horsemen *(of the Apocalypse)* |

James Butler 'Wild Bill' Hickok was a stockman, soldier, spy, deputy US marshall, murderer, sheriff of Ellis County, Ka., marshall of Abilene, Ka., and holder of the most famous hand in poker. When he was shot dead by Jack McCall on 2 August 1876, Wild Bill was holding two black Aces and two black 8s – ever after known as DEADMAN'S HAND. As might be expected from such a legend, considerable dispute surrounds the composition of Hickok's hand, especially the identity of the fifth card or 'kicker'. Most sources agree that the 'kicker' was the 8 of Hearts, but others assert the Jack of Spades, the 9 of Diamonds (see p.56), or even the Queen of Spades.

Forest *('four trees')* | Village People *('four Queens')* | Over & Out | The Devil / The Beast

Oedipus | San Francisco Waiters *('queens with treys')* | Dolly Parton *('working 9–5')* | Pocket Rockets / Bullets

Steel Wheel *(Wheel if unsuited)* | Harry Potter *(J.K. Rowling)* | Ashtray *('ace-trey')* | Pair of Dogs *(two K-9s)*

PLUS-FOURS

Plus-fours are the knicker(bocker)s traditionally favoured by golfers, so named because four extra inches of material were added so that they hung down below the knee. Plus-sixes, plus-eights, and even plus-tens were occasionally sported, though these tended to hinder the follow-through.

—————— BACK TO SQUARE ONE ——————

It is possible that the expression 'back to square one' has its origin in the early days of BBC radio football commentary. In order to help listeners at home follow the live commentary the *Radio Times* printed a schematic of the pitch subdivided into 8 squares (see below). When the ball was passed towards the goal-keeper it went back to square one. The first match to use this diagram was Arsenal *vs* Sheffield, at Highbury, on 22 January 1927.

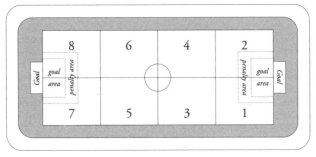

An alternative derivation is that the phrase comes from *Snakes & Ladders*.

—————— THE HOLLYWOOD CRICKET CLUB ——————

The Hollywood Cricket Club was the brainchild of Charles 'Round the Corner' Aubrey Smith (1863–1948) – a right-handed fast bowler who captained England on the 1888–9 tour of South Africa, and was knighted for services to Anglo-American cordiality in 1944. (His nickname derived from a highly idiosyncratic bowling approach, described by W.G. Grace as 'startling'.) Smith was also a Hollywood actor who starred in over 100 pictures, including *Rebecca* (1940) and *Little Women* (1949) – though he tended to be typecast as the archetypal Englishman and even managed to portray the Duke of Wellington in three different films. In 1932, when Smith was living near Mulholland Drive, he persuaded the Los Angeles Park Commission to donate some land on which to build a cricket pitch. Grass seed was imported from England, a pavilion was constructed, and the Aubrey Smith Cricket Field quickly became a mecca for American and ex-pat cricketers. An impressive roll-call of names gained membership of the Club, including Douglas Fairbanks Jr., Cary Grant, David Niven, Basil Rathbone, H.B. Warner, P.G. Wodehouse, Ronald Coleman, and Nigel Bruce – though Smith was not shy in pressurising players to attend. Laurence Olivier was once summoned by note to attend a practice and turned up at nets wearing boots he had borrowed from Boris Karloff.

THE ART OF BULLFIGHTING

Bullfighting is the only art in which the artist is in danger of death and in which the degree of brilliance in the performance is left to the fighter's honour.

— ERNEST HEMINGWAY, *Death in the Afternoon*, 1932

RACKING OF POOL BALLS

UK 8 BALL	9 BALL	US 8 BALL
15 balls are racked in a triangle. The black ball is placed in the centre, and the remaining red and yellow balls are arranged as shown in the diagram below:	9 balls are racked in a diamond formation with the 1-ball at the top, the 9-ball in the centre, and the remaining balls in a random order. For example:	15 balls are racked with the 8-ball in the centre, as below. A stripe must be in one bottom corner, and a solid in the other. The rest are randomly placed. For example:

[The US version of UK 8 BALL is called BLACKBALL and has slightly different racking.]

'SPOOF'

Spoof is a classic pub game of cunning, deception, and guile in which the aim is to be eliminated as quickly as possible. Any convenient number of players sit round a table and surreptitiously place between 0 and 3 coins in one of their hands. When instructed, all place their fist onto the table in front of them. Then, the participants take it in turn to guess the *total* number of coins held in *all* of the hands (usually, the tallest guesses first, and the guessing then rotates anti-clockwise). In a group of five players, for example, the guesses can range between 0 and 15. Importantly, no one may guess the same figure as another. When all have guessed, the coins are revealed and the player who has correctly estimated the total drops out. The game continues until there is only one player left – the loser.

———————— SOME NOTABLE SLEEPERS ————————

❦ The Greek poet EPIMENIDES, is said to have fallen asleep in a cave as a child, and not to have awoken for fifty-seven years, after which he found himself possessed of all wisdom. ❦ In Washington Irving's 1819 story RIP VAN WINKLE slept for twenty years in the Catskill Mountains, waking an old man, 'unknowing and unknown'. ❦ Arthurian Legend tells of MERLIN, who is not dead, but asleep in the form of an old tree yet to wake; and KING ARTHUR himself, who is not dead in Avalon, but is sleeping in the form of a raven. (Incidentally, some say that Merlin was responsible for waking ST DAVID, who was enchanted into sleep for seven years by Ormandine.) ❦ DOG SLEEP, CAT SLEEP, FOX SLEEP, and WEASEL SLEEP are all feigned sleeps taken with one eye metaphorically open. ❦ German mythology tells of CHARLES V, who is asleep until it is time to awake and reclaim his monarchy, and BARBAROSSA, who sleeps with six knights until they are ready to awake and establish Germany as the most powerful state on Earth. ❦ It is said that ST EUTHYMUS slept standing against a wall, and ARSENUS hardly slept at all. ❦ MARGARET THATCHER famously thrived on three or four hours' sleep a night, as did NAPOLEON and the Chinese Communist ZHOU ENLAI. BENJAMIN FRANKLIN once declared: 'Up, sluggard, and waste not life; in the grave will be sleeping enough'. In contrast, HAROLD WILSON said 'I believe the greatest asset a head of state can have is the ability to get a good night's sleep'. ❦ The SEVEN SLEEPERS OF EPHESUS were persecuted Christians who sought refuge in a cave at the time of the Emperor Decius (AD250), and slept for 200 years. They awoke in AD447 during the reign of Theodosius II. ❦ The story of SLEEPING BEAUTY, popularised by Charles Perrault (1628–1703), tells of a beautiful princess cursed by a wicked fairy to prick her finger and die. Fortunately, a good fairy commutes this death sentence into sleep lasting 100 years, from which the princess is released by the kiss of a handsome prince. ❦ Irish legend tells of DESMOND OF KILMALLOCK, who is not dead but asleep in the icy waters of Lough Gur, Limerick. It is said that once each year Desmond awakes and rides in full armour around the Lough before returning to his deep slumber. ❦ A SLEEPLESS HAT is one that is so worn-out it has no nap. ❦ It is said that CHARLEMAGNE is not dead but asleep near Salzburg, waiting for the rise of the Antichrist, at which time he will awaken, conquer evil, and herald the return of Christ. ❦ In Greek mythology, ENDYMION was a handsome shepherd who, while tending flocks on Mount Latmos one night, was spotted sleeping naked by the moon-goddess Selene. Instantly falling in love, Selene flew to Earth in a chariot of silver, and made sweet, sweet love with him. Becoming jealous of his beauty, Selene kissed Endymion's eyes and condemned him to a dreamless sleep during which he would never age. ❦ MORPHEUS is the god of dreams (the son of Somnus, or Hypnos, the ancient god of sleep), after whom the narcotic morphine is named. ❦

THE PALIO OF SIENA

Twice a year, in July and August, ten horses are raced bareback three times around the *Piazza del Campo* in the Italian city of Siena. The race itself lasts only 90 seconds – a fleeting duration which belies the history, pride, and passion that suffuse the event. The contest is known as the *Palio* – which is also the name of the silk standard for which the race is run. *Palios* have taken place in Siena since at least 1238, and only seismic events like cholera, earthquakes, rioting, and war have been allowed to interfere. (Although, in 1919, when rioting was sweeping across the rest of Italy, Siena was curiously peaceful during the *Palio* season.) The key to the *Palio* lies in the structure of Siena, which is divided into *contrade* that act as small social, political, and (historically) military units. In the C14th there were at least 42 *contrade*, but since 1729 there have been just 17:

The division of Siena into its 17 contrade (the numbers correspond to the table opposite); and a schematic of the Piazza del Campo, showing the direction taken by the Palio riders.

The *contrade* are defined by well-established (though invisible) borders which criss-cross the city – each has its own government, motto, saint, emblem, colours, museum, lucky number, and so on. The pride of a *contrada* depends absolutely upon the outcome of each *Palio*. To win a race brings honour and delight; to lose, shame and sadness. Indeed, to come second is considered a far greater humiliation than coming last. Furthermore, a *contrada* allied to the winner will share in its victory; and the winning *contrada's* traditional rival will be considered to have lost, even if they did not race. It is hard to overstate the complexity of the *Palio*, every facet of which is charged with tradition, superstition, and competitive suspicion from selecting which ten *contrade* will race, to allocating each *contrada* a horse. Before each race every horse is taken by its *contrada* into their church to be blessed, after which the horses are carefully guarded to prevent attack from rival *contrade*. During the race itself the jockeys *(fatini)* hold no quarter in intimidating the competition, not least with their *nerbo* – 2½-foot-long whips made from the stretched phalluses of unweaned calves. Once the race is over, the crowds that packed every spare foot of the Piazza mob the winning jockey and horse, scrambling to touch the silk *Palio* itself. This signals the commencement of the celebrations and commiserations which then engulf Siena for days.

The pride of *contrada* membership is fierce and, just as some Yorkshiremen would insist their sons be born in the county to ensure their eligibility for the Yorkshire cricket team, so many Sienese would travel across Italy so that their children might be born in the correct *contrada*. Tabulated below are some of the distinctive features of each of the seventeen *contrade*:

Name	Translation	Associated trade	Colours	Saint's Day	Rivals	Allies	Motto	Wins
1 .. AQUILA†	eagle	notaries	y-lb-bla	Sep 8	13	5,4	From the eagle, beak, claw, and wing	24
2 ... BRUCO†	caterpillar	silk workers	y-lb-g	Jul 2		7,10,16	My name rings out like a revolution	35
3 ... CHIOCCIOLA	snail	tanners	y-t-r	Jun 29	15	7,13,14	Slowly and surely will the Snail win	50
4 .. CIVETTA	owl	cobblers	bla-r-w	Jun 13	8	1,6,7,13	I see through the night	32
5 ... DRAGO	dragon	bankers	r-y-g	Apr 29		1	Fire in my heart becomes flame in my mouth	36
6 ... GIRAFFA	giraffe	painters	w-r	July		4,7,13	The higher the head, the greater the glory	33
7 ... ISTRICE	porcupine	smiths	w-r-bla-bl	Aug 24	9	2,3,4,6	I prick out of defence	40
8 .. LEOCORNO	unicorn	goldsmiths	w-o-t	Jun 24	4	13,15	The arm I bear wounds and heals equally	28
9 .. LUPA	she-wolf	bakers	o-bla-w	Aug 16	7		Et urbis et tenarum signum et decus	34
10 .. NICCHIO†	shell	potters	lb-y-r	Aug 7	17	2,12,15	The red of the coral burns in my heart	42
11 .. OCA†	goose	dyers	w-g-r	Apr 29	16		Clangit ad arma	61
12 .. ONDA	wave	carpenters	w-lb	Jul 2	16	10,15,17	The colour of sky, the strength of ocean	37.5
13 .. PANTERA	panther	apothecaries	r-w-lb	Aug 29	1	3,4,6,8	The panther roared, the people were afraid	25
14 .. SELVA	forest	weavers	g-o-w	Aug 15		3,15	The first forest in the Campo	33
15 .. TARTUCA	tortoise	stonemasons	y-t	Jun 13	3	8,10,12,14	Strength and consistency	44.5
16 .. TORRE	tower	wool carders	r-w-lb	Jul 25	11,12	2	Alongside strength, power	43
17 .. MONTONE	ram	silk merchants	r-y-w	Apr 26	10	12	Walls crumble under my horns	43

Contrade have only been numbered to facilitate identification of allied and rival *contrade*, and for the map opposite. · *Number of wins, as of 2004.*
Colour code: Red, Light Blue, Dark Blue, Yellow, White, Green, Black, Turquoise, Orange, Blue, Pink
† Indicates one of the 'Noble Contrade', so called because of royal recognition

———————— SLEEP AND ITS STAGES ————————

Sleep is generally accepted to be an easily reversed, regular, and natural period of partial or complete unconsciousness, during which the activity of the nervous system is to some degree suspended, the body rests and recuperates, and the individual's responsiveness to their environment is diminished. Although it was long believed that sleep was not uniform, only with the development of the electroencephalogram (EEG), and other electrical tests, were the two main phases or stages of sleep identified:

Non-Rapid-Eye Movement [NREM] sleep has four stages of successive depth *(see the EEG traces opposite)*. It is characterised by a reduction in brain activity, metabolic rate, heart rate, blood-pressure, temperature, and so on. It is thought that NREM sleep is important for growth, energy conservation, and possibly for processing information that was acquired during wakefulness.

Rapid-Eye Movement [REM] sleep is characterised by a reduction in muscle tone, mild involuntary muscle jerks, and the presence of rapid eye movements. REM is the phase when most dreaming takes place, and brain activity increases. In adults, 20–30% of sleep is REM sleep. The function and meaning of dreams are disputed (see p.77).

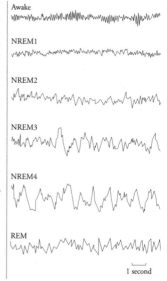

Awake

NREM1

NREM2

NREM3

NREM4

REM

└──┘
1 second

Most sleep begins with NREM1 which lasts roughly 30sec–7min, after which NREM2 takes over, and NREM3 & 4 then occur within 45min or so. Before the first phase of REM we usually return briefly to NREM2. We then tend to alternate between NREM & REM sleep around 4–5 times, at intervals of about 90min; with each alternation the REM period is longer and more intense, and our final sleep stages tend to be NREM2 & REM.

———————— GYMNASTICS EVENTS ————————

MEN · *floor* · *vault* · *pommel-horse* · *parallel bars* · *horizontal bar* · *rings*
WOMEN · *floor exercises* · *vault* · *balance beam* · *asymmetrical bars*

ON WOMEN AND CYCLING

Only a few years ago bicycling was looked upon as a past-time quite unsuited to women. The tricycle was used by a few who felt they needed more vigorous exercise than could be obtained by walking or playing a quiet game of croquet ... But now there is a reaction in its favour and only a few of the obstinately blind are found in opposition ... There is no doubt that the bicycle has brought health to many a nervous, over-wrought woman. All depends, of course, on the common sense displayed by the individual ... No woman should ride if she has any serious weakness, except with great caution, and the permission of a doctor who not only understands her constitution, but who has also made a special study of cycling in all its phases.

— SUSAN, COUNTESS OF MALMESBURY, 1897

A GLOSSARY OF SOME DARTS TERMS

Annie's room	number 1
Bag o' nuts *or* Cup and saucer	a score of 45
Basement	double 3
Bed and breakfast†	26 made up of 5, 20, and 1
Bucket of nails	three 1s
Diddle for the middle	when the closest to the bullseye starts
Double top	double 20
Downstairs	the numbers on the lower half of the board
Feathers	a score of 33
Lord Nelson	a score of 111
Mugs away	when the loser of the last game starts the next
Right church, wrong pew‡	a double of the wrong number
Robin Hood	when a dart sticks into a previous dart
Shanghai	a number, its double, and its triple in three darts
Three in a bed§	three darts in the same number
Ton	a score of 100 or over
Ton-eighty	alternative term for 180
Top of the house	double 20
Upstairs	the numbers on the upper half of the board
X	a double 1 out

† Apparently, a term derived from the days when a stay at a cheap hotel cost just 2*s* 6*d*.
‡ Also, *Right House, Wrong Bed*; *Right Road, Wrong Door*; and *Right Bar, Wrong Barstool*.
§ Devotees of *Bullseye* will recall that two darts in any segment might jeopardise the chance to go through to the finals and maybe, just maybe, win that speed boat. As Tony warned, '*Keep out of the black and into the red, There's nothing in this game for two in a bed!*'

KARATE BELTS

The use of coloured belts to denote experience and status is common to many martial arts, though the exact colour coding varies both across and within disciplines. The convention that the belts get darker as the wearer becomes more qualified has been explained in a number of ways. Some say it is because traditionally the belts were never washed and therefore discoloured with age; others say that the belts were kept and dyed anew. Below is one of the many colour schemes, this one from Shotokan Karate:

Grade	Belt	Japanese
10th Kyu	white	*Soshinsha*
9th Kyu	orange	*Kukyu*
8th Kyu	red	*Hachikyu*
7th Kyu	yellow	*Shichikyu*
6th Kyu	green	*Rokkyu*
5th Kyu	purple	*Gokyu*
4th Kyu	purple & white	*Yonkyu*
3rd Kyu	brown	*Sankyu*
2nd Kyu	brown & white	*Nikyu*
1st Kyu	brown & white	*Ikkyu*
1st Dan	black	*Shodan*
2nd Dan	black	*Nidan*
3rd Dan	black	*Sandan*
4th Dan	black	*Yondan*
5th Dan	black	*Godan*
6th Dan	black	*Rokudan*
7th Dan	black	*Shichidan*
8th Dan	black	*Hachidan*
9th Dan	black	*Kudan*
10th Dan	black	*Judan*

CRICKETING DISMISSALS

Hit Wicket · Caught · Bowled · Run Out · Handled Ball · Stumped
Hit Ball Twice · Timed Out† · Leg Before Wicket · Obstructed Field
† *New batsmen are allowed 3 minutes to get to their crease after the fall of a wicket.*

TOGS & DUVETS

A TOG is a unit of thermal resistance used to express the insulating properties of clothing and bedding. 1 TOG is the resistance that will maintain a temperature difference of 0·1°C with a flux of 1 watt per square metre or, put another way, the TOG value of a textile is equal to 10 times the temperature difference between its two faces when the flow of heat is equal to one watt per square metre. 1 TOG is roughly equal to the thermal resistance of a man's summer suit or a blanket of medium quality; 10 TOGs is the maximum it is practicable to wear. The TOG ratings of duvets vary by manufacturer but, as a rule of thumb, summer duvets are around 4·5–6·0 TOGs, whereas winter duvets have a rating of 12·0–13·5.

The TOG is modelled on the CLO – the insulation required to comfortably maintain a resting subject in a ventilated room (air movement ≈ 10cm/sec) at a temperature of 70°F (21°C), where the prevailing air humidity is less than 50 per cent. 1 TOG ≈ 0.645 CLO.

— 'KABADDI·KABADDI·KABADDI·KABADDI' —

A cross between 'It' and 'British Bulldog', *Kabaddi* is almost certainly the only non-aquatic sport where the ability to hold one's breath is essential. Although the game has a set of well-ordered rules and regulations, some of which are detailed below, the essence of *Kabaddi* is that it can be played almost anywhere, by any group, with no specialist clothing or equipment.

Formal *Kabaddi* courts are 13m × 10m, divided into two halves, each of which is again divided ⅔rds along by *baulk* lines. Because each side fields only 7 players out of a squad of 12, *sitting blocks* are positioned at either end of the court.

Teams take it in turns to send a *raider* into the opposing team's half which is populated by the *anti-raiders* (or *antis*). Before crossing the centre line, the *raiders* must loudly and clearly start to repeat the word *Kabaddi*[†] (over and over again) to demonstrate that they are not breathing in. This repetition is known as the *cant*, and any player who pauses during his *cant* is out. (Players are also out if they cross the court's boundary lines.) Once within the opposing team's half, *raiders* attempt to cross their opponent's *baulk* line and then return home while touching as many of the *antis* as possible. If a *raider* manages this while keeping his *cant* going it is known as a *successful raid*, and all those *antis* who were touched during the *raid* are ruled out. It is the job of the *antis* to *hold* the *raider* and prevent him from returning to his court before his *cant* collapses. Any *raider* who is *held* can get safe if he is able to touch the ground in his home half with any part of his body. When a player is out he must leave the field, and is only *revived* when a member of the opposing team gets out[‡]. Teams score 1 point for each player they put out, and 2 bonus points (a *lona*) for putting out an entire team. A typical games lasts 40 minutes with a 5-minute interval at half time, and games are staged on categories of weight and age. 7 officials are required to police the game of *Kabaddi* – which is also played in a circular arena, when it becomes known as *Amar Kabaddi*.

† Kabaddi has been played under a host of other names that sometimes serve as the basis of the *cant*, including: *do-do-do, zabar gagana, hututu, chedu-gudu, kapati,* and *wandikali*.
‡ A number of variants have different rules for players given out: *sanjeevani*, where, once out, a player can be revived; *amar*, where a player given out can remain on the field, although his out is scored; and *ganimi*, where, once given out, a player cannot be revived.

——— LAZY MAN'S LOAD ———

A *Lazy Man's Load* is one too heavy to be carried; named after indolent types who overload themselves, hoping that they will not need to return.

GOLF IRON LOFT ANGLES

Below are illustrated the standard loft angles of a set of golf irons, along with the average range of male players, female players, and Tiger Woods:

Face profile										
Iron number	2	3	4	5	6	7	8	9	PW	SW
Face angle (c.)	20°	23°	26°	30°	34°	38°	42°	46°	50°	56°
Male (yds)	170-90	160-80	150-70	140-60	130-50	120-40	110-30	100-20	90-110	<100
Female (yds)	150-70	140-60	130-50	120-40	110-30	100-20	90-110	80-100	70-90	<80
Tiger (yds)	245	230	220	210	190	170	160	145	130	110

CHESTERFIELD ON LAZY & TRIFLING MINDS

Below is the distinction that Lord Chesterfield (1694–1773) made (on 26 July 1748) between LAZY and TRIFLING minds in one of the many authoritarian letters of instruction[†] he wrote to his illegitimate son Philip.

'The LAZY MIND will not take the trouble of going to the bottom of anything; but, discouraged by the first difficulties … stops short, contents itself with easy, and consequently superficial knowledge, and prefers a great degree of ignorance to a small degree of trouble …'

'The TRIFLING AND FRIVOLOUS mind is always busied, but to little purpose; it takes little objects for great ones, and throws away upon trifles that time and attention which only important things deserve. Knick-knacks; butterflies; shells, insects, etc., are the subjects of their most serious researches …'

'…For God's sake then reflect. Will you throw this time away either in laziness, or in trifles? … Read only useful books; and never quit a subject till you are thoroughly master of it, but read and inquire on till then.'

† *Samuel Johnson declared of Chesterfield's letters: 'They teach the morals of a whore, and the manners of a dancing master.' This barbed comment was provoked by Chesterfield's failure to live up to his offer of financial patronage while Johnson was compiling his* Dictionary of the English Language. *Johnson took further revenge by defining the word* patron *in his dictionary thus – 'Patron: commonly a wretch who supports with insolence, and is paid with flattery'.*

HANDS, FEET, & HORSES

A HAND is the traditional measure of horses. In the C19th, a HAND was taken as 3 inches (¼ foot), but nowadays 4 inches (⅓ foot) is standard.

NEVADA'S FIGHTING FOULS

Because of the local popularity of toughman, badman, ultimate fighting, and other varieties of mixed martial-art competitions, Nevada State law [NAC 467.7962] details a host of acts that constitute fouls in such contests:

Butting with the head · Eye gouging of any kind · Biting
Hair pulling · Fishhooking · Groin attacks of any kind
Putting a finger into any orifice or into any cut or laceration
Small joint manipulation · Striking to the spine or the back of the head
Striking downward using the point of the elbow
Throat strikes of any kind, including grabbing the trachea
Clawing, pinching or twisting the flesh · Grabbing the clavicle
Kicking or kneeing the head of a grounded opponent
Stomping a grounded opponent · Kicking to the kidney with the heel
Spiking an opponent to the canvas on his head or neck
Throwing an opponent out of the ring or fenced area
Holding the shorts or gloves of an opponent · Spitting at an opponent
Using abusive language in the ring or fenced area
Timidity, including avoiding contact with an opponent, intentionally
or consistently dropping the mouthpiece or faking an injury

'ABIDE WITH ME'

Written by Henry Francis Lyte (1793–1847) in the weeks before he died of tuberculosis, *Abide With Me* has been sung at the FA Cup final ever since 23 April 1927, when Cardiff City beat Arsenal 1–0 at Wembley Stadium:

Abide with me; fast falls the eventide;
The darkness deepens; Lord with me abide.
When other helpers fail and comforts flee,
Help of the helpless, O abide with me.

Swift to its close ebbs out life's little day;
Earth's joys grow dim; its glories pass away;
Change and decay in all around I see;
O Thou who changest not, abide with me.

Not a brief glance I beg, a passing word;
But as Thou dwell'st with Thy disciples, Lord,
Familiar, condescending, patient, free.
Come not to sojourn, but abide with me.

Come not in terrors, as the King of kings,
But kind and good, with healing in Thy wings,
Tears for all woes, a heart for every plea —
Come, Friend of sinners, and thus bide with me.

Thou on my head in early youth didst smile;
And, though rebellious and perverse meanwhile,
Thou hast not left me, oft as I left Thee,
On to the close, O Lord, abide with me.

I need Thy presence every passing hour.
What but Thy grace can foil the tempter's power?
Who, like Thyself, my guide and stay can be?
Through cloud and sunshine, Lord, abide with me.

I fear no foe, with Thee at hand to bless;
Ills have no weight, and tears no bitterness.
Where is death's sting? Where, grave, thy victory?
I triumph still, if Thou abide with me.

Hold Thou Thy cross before my closing eyes;
Shine through the gloom and point me to the skies.
Heaven's morning breaks, and earth's vain shadows flee;
In life, in death, O Lord, abide with me.

The hymn was a favourite of Gandhi, it was sung at the weddings of King George VI and Elizabeth II, and it was played as the *Titanic* went under.

—— SOME SPORTING MEDICAL COMPLAINTS ——

Below are the medical translations for some colloquial sporting injuries:

Arm wrestler's arm......................................radial nerve palsy†
Athlete's foot................fungal disease – epidermophyton floccosum
Athlete's heel..plantar fasciitis
Athlete's groin ....adductor tendinitis
Bunions ....hallux valgus
Cauliflower ear....................subperichondral auricular haematoma
Cheerleader's hand....................median palmar digital neuropathy
Clergyman's throat ....chronic pharyngitis
Climber's elbow..................................medial epicondylitis
Computer-gamer's palm..........................central palmar blister
Computer-gamer's palsy.........................distal ulnar neuropathy
Cyclist's handlebar palsy................................ulnar neuropathy
Golfers' elbow ....medial epicondylitis
Golfer's hip ....trochanteric bursitis
Housemaid's knee ....prepatellar bursitis
Jogger's foot ....medial plantar nerve entrapment
Jogger's nipple ....friction-induced dermatitis with lichenification
Jumper's Knee..patella tendinitis
Pedal pusher's palsy....................................sciatic neuropathy
Pitcher's elbow ....rotator cuff tendinitis
Pitcher's thumb....................................digital nerve neuroma
Punch drunk...................................dementia pugilistica
Road runner's foot...............................calcaneal stress fracture
Rope skipper's thigh ....lateral femoral cutaneous neuropathy
Runner's knee.......................iliotibial band friction syndrome
Runner's stitch ....praecordial catch syndrome
Runner's toe...................................metatarsal stress fracture
Shin splints....................................medial tibial stress syndrome
Snowboarder's ankle...........................fracture of the lateral talus
Squash player's palsy ....tenosynovitis of the extensor pollicis longus
Swimmer's ear...otitis externa
Swimmer's goggle headache ....supraorbital neuropathy
Tennis elbow ....lateral epicondylitis
Tennis leg ....medial head of gastrocnemius rupture
Trigger finger ....stenosing tenosynovitis
Turf toe ....sprain of the first metatarsophalangeal joint
Unicyclist's groin ....sciatic neuropathy
Weightlifter's shoulder ....suprascapular neuropathy
Yoga guru's footdrop‡..............common peroneal nerve compression

† The radial nerve can also be damaged by prolonged or inappropriate use of handcuffs.
‡ Also known as 'strawberry picker's footdrop'. · (See *Focal Dystonia, Yips, &c.* on p.28.)

WODEHOUSE ON CROSSWORDS

To a man who has been beating his head against the wall for twenty minutes over a single anagram, it is g. and wormwood to read that the Provost of Eton measures the time needed to boil his breakfast egg by the time needed to solve *The Times* crossword – and the Provost hates his eggs hard-boiled.

— P.G. WODEHOUSE

LAS VEGAS CASINO HIERARCHY

TABLE GAMES	SLOT MACHINES
DEALER	CHANGE GIRL
STICKMAN (craps)	CAROUSEL ATTENDENT
BOXMAN	FLOORMAN
FLOORMAN	ASSISTANT SHIFT MANAGER
PIT BOSS	SHIFT MANAGER
GAMES SHIFT MANAGER	DIRECTOR OF SLOTS
CASINO MANAGER	GENERAL MANAGER
GENERAL MANAGER	

THREE CARD MONTE

Three Card Monte – otherwise known as *Find the Lady* or *Bonneteau* – is one of the oldest scams. Three cards, usually two black cards and a red Queen, are placed (by the *tosser*) on a table and shuffled before your eyes. You have to find the lady. Although to most players it seems that only the *tosser* is involved, all such scams employ *ropers* who crowd the table, *shills* who pretend to be winning punters, and *scouts* who keep a look-out for the law. Sometimes the *shills* or *ropers* will 'help' a punter by covertly turning down the corner of the Queen when the *tosser* is not looking – only for the *tosser* to sneakily straighten that card and bend the corner of another. Clearly, the only reliable way to win this game is never to play. However, if you are tempted, the best advice is this: follow the dealer's hands very closely until you are absolutely certain beyond any doubt that you have identified the Queen. Then, bet on one of the other two cards, thus increasing your chance of winning from zero to fifty per cent. That said, if by chance you do win there is a high probability that a *scout* will raise the alarm and the game will be abandoned before you have collected your money, or that you will be pursued and 'relieved' of your winnings.

————————CRYPTIC CROSSWORD CODES————————

A few abbreviations and codes commonly used in cryptic crossword clues:

Anagram 'signposts' are often used to indicate an anagram is in the clue:
torn · scrambled · confused · wild · exploding · twisted · improved · new shuffle(d) · shaken · reform(ed) · jumbled · drunken · unusual · badly · etc.

clue	possible interpretation		
sailor	AB; jack; tar; salt; rating	football	FA
flower	river	mother	ma; mom
asleep; snoring; dreaming	zz	ship	ss
nil; duck; love; zero	o	way; road	rd, ave, st, lane
horse	gg; nag	the French	le; la
abstainer	tt	of German	der; die; das
posh; upper class	U	the Spanish	el
bible; testaments	OT; NT	of French	de
journalist	ed(itor)	model; car; ford	t
spies; spooks	CIA	worker	ant; bee; drone
soldiers	GI; TA; RE; RA; etc.	holy man	st
painter	RA; rope	short time	min, hr, sec, tim
rugby	RU	bloomer	flower
		worker	ant

Days of the week .... ((M)on)day; ((W)ed)nesday; etc.
Months of the year .... ((J)an)uary; ((F)eb)ruary; etc.
Compass point (directions).... (N)orth; (S)outh; (N)orth (E)asterly; etc.
Weights and measures...... (K)ilo; (G)ramme; (T)onne; (lb) pound; etc.
Musical abbreviations........... *piano* (p) soft(ly); *forte* (f) loud(ly); etc.
Military ranks .... CO; NCO; (GEN)eral; (COL)onel; etc.
Playing cards ... (Q)ueen; (J)ack; (K)nave; (K)ing; hearts; diamonds; etc.
American States .... NY; PA; CI; CA; TX; etc.
Country codes .... UK; GB; NI; USA; UN; FRA; etc.
Chemical symbols..... Gold (Au) or 'ore'; Copper (Cu); Silver (Ag); etc.

Numerals	IV	4	VIII	8	XV	15	D	500
I	1	V	5	IX	9	L	50	M	1000
II	2	VI	6	X	10	LX	60	MD	1500
III	3	VII	7	XI	11	C	100	MM	2000

Some abbreviations		ie	that is	(G)PO	post office
eg	for example	nb	note	is	island
PC	policeman	YR	year(ly)	r	road
MD; GP	doctor	RN	Royal Navy	o	ring; hole
MP	politician	X	cross; kiss; love	ng	no good
CE	Church of Eng.	c	circa; century	ac	accountant

INTERNATIONAL PLAYING CARD PACKS

Country	Suits	Court cards	Numerals	Standard deck
GERMAN	leaves, acorns, hearts, bells	King, Over, Under	7, 8, 9, 10, Ace	32
SWISS	shields, acorns, flowers, bells	King, Over, Under	6, 7, 8, 9, 10, Deuce	36
SPANISH	swords, clubs, cups, coins	King, Knight, Valet	1, 2, 3, 4, 5, 6, 7	40
ITALIAN	swords, batons, cups, coins	King, Knight, Footsoldier	1, 2, 3, 4, 5, 6, 7	40
FRENCH	spades, clubs, hearts, diamonds	King, Queen, Knave	Ace, 2, 3, 4, 5, 6, 7, 8, 9, 10	52

THE FIVE 'CLASSICS' & OTHER INTERNATIONAL RACES OF NOTE

Classic Race	Open to	Distance	Location	Month	1st Race	1st Winner
The 2000 Guineas	3 y/o colts & fillies	1 mile	Newmarket	May	1809	Wizard
The 1000 Guineas	3 y/o fillies	1 mile	Newmarket	May	1814	Charlotte
The Oaks	3 y/o fillies	1 mile 4 furlongs 10 yards	Epsom	June	1779	Bridget
The Derby	3 y/o colts & fillies	1 mile 4 furlongs 10 yards	Epsom	June	1780	Diomed
The St Leger	3 y/o colts & fillies	1 mile 6 furlongs 132 yards	Doncaster	September	1776	Allabaculia

Race	Country	Distance	Location	Month	1st Race	1st Winner
Prix de l'Arc de Triomphe	France	1½ miles	Longchamp	October	1920	Comrade
Kentucky Derby	USA	1¼ miles	Churchill Downs	May	1875	Aristides
Melbourne Cup	Australia	3,200 metres	Flemington Park	November	1861	Archer
Irish Derby	Ireland	1½ miles	Curragh	June	1866	Selim
Dubai World Cup	UAE	1 mile 2 furlongs	Nad Al Sheba	March	1996	Cigar
Queen's Plate	Canada	1¼ miles	Woodbine	July	1860	Don Juan

—————— AN ANGLER'S CALENDAR ——————

Angling may be said to be so like the mathematics,
that it can never be fully learnt.
— IZAAK WALTON, *The Compleat Angler*, 1653

This angling calendar is from an untitled German text (*c.*1493) by van der Goes, translated in 1872 into English and Flemish by Alfred Denison:

The SALMON in April and May, and a little while after it is at its very best and the salmon remains so till the day of St James. Then it must be left to St Andrew's Day and it is best between St Michael's Mass and St Martin's.

The PIKE is best in July, only the pike is good at all times, only excepted when he sees the rye he spawns.

The forepart of a PIKE or CARP is better always than the hind part, it is the same with other fishes.

A TENCH is always best in June.

The PERCH is always good except in May or April.

The BREAM and MACKEREL are good in February and March.

The MULLET is good in March or April.

A KULLUNCK is best at Candlemas Day and continues good in April.

The RUDD is good in February and March and falls off in May.

The GUDGEONS are good in February, March, and April, till May. Only the young Gudgeon is always good with parsley.

A BLEAK is best in Autumn.

The STICKLEBACKS are good in March, and in the beginning of May, when they are full they shall be stirred with eggs.

The EEL is good in May till the day of the Assumption of Our Lady.

A LAMPREY is never better than in May.

A LAMPHERN, the brother of the lamprey, is good from the thirteenth Mass to the day of Our Lady's Annunciation.

The CRAYFISH is best in March and April and particularly when the moon increases, then they are so much the better.

Fly-fishing may be a very pleasant amusement;
but angling or float-fishing I can only compare to a stick and a string,
with a worm at one end and a fool at the other.
— SAMUEL JOHNSON [attrib.]

HOUDINI'S CODE

Harry Houdini created an elaborate code with his wife-cum-glamorous-assistant Bess to perform 'mind reading' illusions involving numbers. Bess would indicate, say, the serial number of a dollar bill, or a punter's date of birth, by constructing a sentence utilising the following code words:

1 . . . . pray	3 . . . . say	5 . . . . tell	7 . . . . . speak	9 . . . . . . look
2 . . . . answer	4 . . . . . . now	6 . . . . . please	8 . . . . quickly	0 . . be quick

For example the driving licence number 4785932 would be revealed by:

Now! Speak to me, oh great Houdini! Quickly tell me!
Look deep within your mind, and say the answer!

DRINKING GAME ADMINISTRATION

It is outside the scope of this *Miscellany* to detail the many and various drinking games which exist (e.g. *ibble-dibble, bunnies,* or *drink while you think*). However, a few organisational and administrative customs and traditions seem to be common to most drinking games around the world:

MR CHAIRMAN · In sole charge of setting and enforcing all rules and fines. All conversations must go 'through' the Chairman. When the Chairman drinks, everyone drinks.

MR WEIGHTS & MEASURES · In charge of ensuring that all have adequate drinks, and that any fines levied are completely consumed. He is particularly concerned with short measures and 'spillage'.

MR CHIEF SNEAK · Reports any rule-breaking to the Chairman.

THUMB MASTER · If at any time the Thumb Master places his thumb on the edge of the table, every other player must follow suit. The last player to notice and place his thumb is fined.

POINTING is forbidden. Only elbows may be used to indicate. Only LEFT-HANDED DRINKING is usually permitted. Some play the rule known as HALF HOUR HAND when the drinking hand changes every thirty minutes. FIRST NAMES are replaced by surnames or nicknames. SWEARING is forbidden. Drinks that are placed perilously close to the edge of a table (say a finger's length) may be deemed by the CHIEF SNEAK to be DANGEROUS PINTS – and must be imbibed forthwith. Certain words are prohibited and must be replaced by synonyms: drinks are TIPPLES or BEVERAGES, and drinking is IMBIBING; the bar is the SALOON; fingers are DIGITS; etc. If a COIN is dropped into a glass, its contents must be finished.

———————— ON IDLENESS & IDLERS ————————

SAMUEL JOHNSON · If you are idle, be not solitary; if you are solitary, be not idle.

HENRY FORD · There is no place in civilisation for the idler. None of us has any right to ease.

ST MATTHEW · Every idle word that men shall speak, they shall give account thereof in the day of judgement.

OSCAR WILDE · The condition of perfection is idleness.

THOMAS PYNCHON · Writers of course are the mavens of sloth … Idle dreaming is often the essence of what we do.

SOMERSET MAUGHAM · It was such a lovely day. I thought it was a pity to get up.

LORD CRANBORNE · [on Kenneth Clark MP] One of the reasons he would be good is that he is idle. There is a lot to be said for idle leaders (see also p.85).

GEORGE ELIOT · There's many a one who would be idle if hunger didn't pinch him; but the stomach sets us to work.

OSCAR WILDE · I feel an irresistible desire to wander, and go to Japan, where I will pass my youth, sitting under an almond tree, drinking amber tea out of a blue cup, and looking at a landscape without perspective.

THOMAS À KEMPIS · *Numquam sis ex toto otiosus, sed aut legens, aut scribens, aut orans, aut meditans, aut aliquid utilitatis pro communi laborans.* [Never be completely idle, but either reading, or writing, or praying, or meditating, or at some useful work for the common good.]

SAMUEL JOHNSON · We would all be idle if we could.

JEAN JACQUES ROUSSEAU · I love to busy myself about trifles, to begin a hundred things and not finish one of them … in short to fritter the whole day away inconsequentially … and to follow nothing but the whim of the moment.

SPANISH PROVERB · How perfect it is to do nothing, and then afterwards rest.

JEROME K. JEROME · There are plenty of lazy people and plenty of slowcoaches, but a genuine idler is a rarity.

LORENZO DI COMO · An idle life is a prize to be laboured for; to be idle is the quintessence of life.

D.E. McCONNELL · Perhaps the greatest cause of misery and wretchedness in social life is idleness. The want of something to do is what makes people wicked and miserable. It breeds selfishness, mischief-making, envy, jealousy and vice, in all its most dreadful forms.

———————— ON IDLENESS & IDLERS cont. ————————

JAMES THURBER · It is better to have loafed and lost than never to have loafed at all.

W.F. HARGREAVES ·
  I'm Burlington Bertie,
  I rise at ten-thirty
  And saunter along like a toff.
  I walk down the Strand
  With my gloves on my hand,
  Then I walk down again
    with them off.
(See also p.32 and p.42.)

LORD CHESTERFIELD · Idleness is only the refuge of weak minds. (See also p.92.)

ISAAC WATTS · Tis the voice of the sluggard, I heard him complain: 'You have waked me too soon, I must slumber again.'

SAMUEL JOHNSON · I have, all my life long, been lying till noon; yet I tell all young men, and tell them with great sincerity, that nobody who does not rise early will ever do any good.

F. SCOTT FITZGERALD · Sometimes I think that idlers seem to be a special class for whom nothing can be planned, plead as one will with them ...

CHINESE PROVERB · It has ever been thus, that young idlers make old penitents.

JEROME K. JEROME · I like work; it fascinates me. I can sit and look at it for hours. I love to keep it by me; the idea of getting rid of it nearly breaks my heart.

———————— SOME ENDURANCE RACES ————————

Race	*description of the madness*
Marathon des Sables†	*151-mile race run over 6 days in the Sahara*
Everest Marathon	*marathon at an altitude of 5,184m*
South-pole ultramarathon	*45km race in snow shoes to the South Pole*
Badwater	*135 miles from Death Valley to Mount Whitney*
Cornbelt Run	*run continuously for 24 hours round a 400m track*
JFK Ultra	*50 miles with over 800 competitors*
Comrades Marathon	*Durban to Pietermaritzburg, 89km*
Devil o' the Highlands	*43 miles up and down Scottish mountains*
Jungle Run	*200km over 7 days through the Amazon jungle*
Self-transcendence race	*longest foot race in the world, 3,100 miles*
Spartathlon	*historical race, run from Athens to Sparta, 246km*
Escarpment trail	*30km mountain race over the Catskill mountains*
Gobi March	*7-day, 155-mile race across the Gobi desert*

† During this marathon a camel ensures that only those able to keep up can continue. The camel plods along behind the race, and any runner passed by the beast is disqualified.

—————BALLROOM DANCING TIMES & TEMPOS—————

dance	time	tempo
Waltz	3/4	bpm 30
Foxtrot	4/4	30
Quickstep	4/4	52
Tango	2/4	33
Viennese Waltz	3/4	60

Rumba	4/4	27
Samba	2/4	52
Cha Cha Cha	4/4	32
Paso Doble	2/4	62
Jive	4/4	44

[International Dancesport Federation]

————— NINE MEN'S MORRIS · MERELLES —————

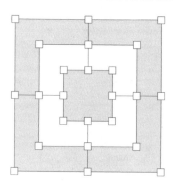

In turn, players lay one of their 9 men on the board's intersecting points: the aim is to get 3 men in a row (a MILL). When a player makes a MILL they can remove 1 of their opponent's men from the board (so long as it is not part of a MILL and there are other available men). Once all the men are down, they can be moved along lines to adjacent points. The game ends when a player has only 2 men, or when a player can't make a move.

—————SOME BOXING NICKNAMES—————

Jack *'The Lancashire Hero'* Carpenter · Ray *'Boom Boom'* Mancini
Bishop *'The Bold Smuggler'* Sharpe · *'Iron'* Mike Tyson
Alec *'The Chelsea Snob'* Reid · Tom *'The Bath Carpenter'* Gaynor
'Marvelous' Marvin Hagler[†] · Tommy *'The Hitman'* Hearns
Rocky *'The Italian Stallion'* Balboa (see p.35) · Jake *'Raging Bull'* LaMotta
Roberto *'Hands of Stone'* Duran · *'Smokin''* Joe Frazier
Apollo *'The Count of Monte Fisto'* Creed (see p.35)
Vinny *'The Pazmanian Devil'* Pazienza
Joe *'The Brown Bomber'* Louis · *'Prince'* Naseem Hamed
Oscar *'The Golden Boy'* de la Hoya
Tommy *'The Tonypandy Terror'* Farr
Larry *'The Easton Assassin'* Holmes · Donovan *'Razor'* Ruddock
Peter *'Young Rump Steak'* Crawley · James *'Bonecrusher'* Smith

† Marvin Hagler was the undisputed World Middleweight Champion from 1980–7, winning 13 of his 15 world title fights, and losing only to *'Sugar'* Ray Leonard. Marvin was so proud of his monicker that he actually had his name legally changed to Marvelous.

—TYPOLOGY OF COMPETITIVE BOOMERANG—

Across the world, notably in Australia and America, boomerangs are thrown competitively in a number of different events, some of which are:

ACCURACY · throws are made from the centre of a set of circles marked on the ground. Points are awarded for how close it lands to the bullseye.

TRICK CATCH · for example, one-handed, behind the back, under the leg, caught with feet, and so on. (Tricks are also performed with two boomerangs simultaneously.)

AUSTRALIAN ROUND · tests the distance of the throw, the accuracy of the return, and the skill of the catch over five attempts.

FAST CATCH · making five throws and catches as quickly as possible with the same boomerang.

ENDURANCE · involves making as many throws as possible over a five-minute period.

DOUBLES · throwing and catching two boomerangs at the same time.

MAXIMUM TIME ALOFT [MTA] · the longest of five throws to stay in the air – the current record is 17 minutes 6 seconds by John Gorski, in Ohio on 8 August 1993.

JUGGLING · keeping two or more boomerangs in the air at the same time for as long as possible.

LONG DISTANCE · where points are awarded on distance thrown.

FREESTYLE · where points are awarded for height, speed, style, and general finesse.

Many of these events are played as team events, usually with four members per team. One team event involves three players playing FAST CATCH for the time that the fourth plays MTA.

[Most standard boomerang events require each boomerang to fly a minimum of 20 metres out from the throw to be counted.]

— SOME PREFERRED COARSE FISHING BAITS —

Bait	*Type of fish*	Bait	Type of fish
Hempseed	Roach	Bread paste	Barbel & tench
Dog-biscuits	Carp & chub	Lob worms	Perch
Sweetcorn	Carp, barbel, & tench	Marshmallows	Carp
Spam	Chub, barbel, & carp	Casters‡	Dace, roach, & chub
Cheese	Chub	Maggots	Most fish
Boilies†	Carp	Slugs	Chub
		Cat food	Carp

† Balls of paste mixed with egg and boiled into hard pellets, so small fish cannot nibble.
‡ Chrysalis stage of maggots. · [Clearly such a table can only hope to annoy fishermen.]

CABER TOSSING

Tossing the caber is a key element of any Highland Games. The caber itself is a tree trunk (denuded of its branches) of unspecified size – though it has to be of a length and weight to challenge even the strongest athlete. (Occasionally, cabers are submerged overnight in nearby lochs to increase their weight.) Athletes are presented with the caber in its vertical position, and their challenge is to upend the trunk in a perfect longitudinal revolution, so that the caber's top faces them. A perfect toss should land directly in front of the tosser, at '12 o'clock', without deviating to the right or left. Tossers are given three attempts with a caber – of which the best throw is scored. If a new caber cannot be tossed it may be progressively shortened until an athlete is successful, after which the caber may never be modified. Perhaps the most famous challenge is presented by the Braemar Caber which weighs 54·5kg (120lb) and is 5·79m (19ft) long. It was first successfully tossed by 51-year-old George Clark in 1951.

JOIN-THE-DOT PUZZLES

The 16 circles can be joined with 6 straight lines; the 9 squares can be joined with 4 straight lines. (In both cases the lines must be continuous.)
For solutions, turn to p.160.

THE FIFTEEN POINTS OF A GOOD HORSE

Wynkyn de Worde (d.1535) was an Alsatian-born pioneer of printing. He was employed at William Caxton's London press, and took control of the business when Caxton died in 1491. De Worde was the first printer in England to employ italic typefaces. In one of the many publications he printed de Worde enumerated the fifteen points required of a good horse:

A good horse sholde have three propyrtees of a man, three of a woman, three of a foxe, three of a haare, and three of an asse.

Of a MAN. Bolde, prowde, and hardye.
Of a WOMAN. Fayre-breasted, faire of heere, and easy to move.
Of a FOXE. A fair taylle, short eers, with a good trotte.
Of a HAARE. A grate eye, a dry head, and well rennynge.
Of an ASSE. A bygge chynn, a flat legge, and a good hoof.

SOME GAMBLING TERMINOLOGY

Action..... the amount of money in a pot; a high-rolling gambling table
Anchor man .... the player, to the right of the dealer, who plays last
Ante .... a sum paid into the pot before the game starts
Bad beat .... snatching defeat from the jaws of victory
Beard .... a runner for a gambler who wants to remain anonymous
Bet the pot .... to bet a sum equal to that in the pot
Bones .... colloquialism for dice or dominoes
Bottom deal .... a (crooked) deal from the bottom of the deck
Burned cards .... cards discarded from a pack before dealing
Call .... in poker, to match the last bet
Carte blanche .... a hand of cards with no face-card
Chalk .... a favourite
Churn .... betting with money you have won (until you lose)
Cold (*or* stacked) deck .... a pre-ordered rigged pack of cards
Comp .... 'free' incentives given by the House to high rollers[†]
Court card .... King, Queen, Jack (see p.34)
Doublet .... a domino with the same value at each end
Edge .... the statistical advantage the House enjoys in each game
Faites vos jeux .... Place your bets
Fishing .... remaining in a card game in the hope of a vital card
Frenchies .... ostensibly honest players who will cheat if need be
Hold your own .... break-even
Juice .... the profit made by the House
Lines .... odds
Parlay .... a bet which depends on a series of propositions occurring
Press .... to increase one's original stake
Pressing .... adding money just won to the next bet
Rien ne va plus .... No more bets
Runt .... a poker hand worth less than a pair
Rush .... a winning streak
Soft hand .... a blackjack hand where an Ace is counted as 11
Steal .... to win a game by bluffing; or, simply, to steal
Stock .... the undealt cards
Talon .... the pile of discarded cards
Toke .... to tip the dealer
Trey .... a 3 of any suit in cards
Underlay .... a bad or 'unlucky' bet
Vig (*or* vigorish) .... the percentage of any House or bookmaker
Welsh (welch) .... to fail to repay a debt
Yarborough .... a whist or bridge hand with no card higher than a 9

[†] A classic American *comp* term popular in Las Vegas is 'RFB' which stands for Room, Food & Beverages. · (See also Craps, p.14; Dice Odds, p.106; and Rigged Dice, p.116.)

—OLYMPIC HORSE COLOUR NOMENCLATURE—

The colour codes for horses entered into Olympic equestrian events are:

DU .... Dun	PA .... Palomina	PB .... Piebald
AP .... Appaloosa	GR .... Grey	LB......... Light Bay
BA............... Bay	CH......... Chestnut	DC.. Dark Chestnut
BL .... Black	DB......... Dark Bay	RO .... Roan

——— TWO DICE ODDS ———

no.	ways		probability	odds
12	1	*(box cars)*	0·0278	35/1
11	2		0·0556	17/1
10	3		0·0833	11/1
9	4		0·1111	8/1
8	5		0·1389	31/5
7	6		0·1667	5/1
6	5		0·1389	31/5
5	4		0·1111	8/1
4	3		0·0833	11/1
3	2		0·0556	17/1
2	1	*(snake eyes)*	0·0278	35/1

A score achieved by rolling 2 identical dice (e.g. a total of 6 with 3/3 rather than 4/2 or 5/1) is considered to have been made the 'hard way'. Here, the odds expressed are those that would be given by a bookmaker: 35/1 = 1 in 36.

——— RULE 27 ———

Rule 27 was passed in 1902 by the Gaelic Athletic Association (GAA) in response to a wave of Irish nationalism. The Rule prohibited any member of the GAA from playing, attending, or promoting any 'English' sport – such as rugby, soccer, hockey, or cricket. Anyone breaching 'The Ban' (as Rule 27 became known) would be suspended. The most controversial suspension came in 1938 when no less than the President of Ireland, Dr Douglas Hyde, was sacked as patron of the GAA. Dr Hyde, a passionate supporter of Irish culture and language, had been required to attend an international soccer match in his capacity as President. Over time the validity of the Rule was increasingly called into question and by the 1950s the Ban was honoured more in the breach than in the observance. In 1968 a report was commissioned to examine the political situation, and at the 1971 GAA Congress 28 of the 32 counties voted to abolish Rule 27.

BOULE, BUTTOCKS, & FANNY

Boule tradition dictates that if a team fails to score a single point during a match they are expected to kneel and kiss the bare buttocks of the legendary voluptuary 'Fanny' *(rotondités de la plantureuse Fanny)*, whose image is to be found on pictures and sculptures in many a boule club.

SKI RUN DIFFICULTY · PISTE COLOURS

Area	Easiest	Medium	Hard	Hardest
Europe	*(green†)*	*blue*	*red*	*black*
North America	*green* ○	*blue* □	*black* ◊	*black* ◊◊
South America	*green*	*blue*	*red*	*black*
Japan	*green*	*green*	*red*	*black*
Australia, New Zealand	*green*	*blue*	*black*	*black*

† Green tends to be used in France. · [The grading of runs is often left to the discretion of individual resorts, and commercial pressures can influence how runs are graded. For example, there is a temptation to upgrade runs to black for reasons of prestige and, conversely, some runs that return skiers to their accommodation are downgraded to make them more acceptable to families. Runs marked with broken black, red, or broken yellow and black lines may signify 'itineraried runs', which are semi-official off-piste runs, usually of a difficult black grade, which tend to be patrolled, but not necessarily 'pisted'.]

SHUTTLECOCKS

Shuttlecocks have 16 feathers fixed into a cork base. These feathers† are taken from duck or white goose and must be 64–70mm long; the tips of the feathers should form a circle with a diameter of 58–68mm; the base should be rounded at the bottom with a diameter of 25–28mm; the shuttlecock should weigh 4.74–5.50g. Shuttlecocks are classified thus:

Speed	weight	grain	for use
Slow	4.8g	75	at altitude
Medium slow	4.9g	76	in hot climates
Medium	5g	77	at sea-level
Medium fast	5.1g	78	in cold climates
Fast	5.2g	79	below sea-level

Each classification adds approximately 30cm to the distance travelled‡. Grains are an alternative measure of weight used by manufacturers; 7,000 grains weigh approximately 1lb.

† Feathers from both wings are used, but the best shuttlecocks use feathers from only one side. Feathers from the left wing are said to be more stable in flight. ‡To test the flight of a shuttlecock, stand on the back line and hit it with a underhand stroke. A good shuttlecock will land not less that 530mm or more than 990mm short of the opposite back line.

——————— ON GOD AND DICE ———————

God's dice always have a lucky roll.
— SOPHOCLES (497–406BC)

The devil invented dice.
— ST AUGUSTINE (AD354–430)

The dice of God are always loaded.
— RALPH WALDO EMERSON (1803–82)

God does not play dice with the Universe.
— ALBERT EINSTEIN (1879–1955), objecting to quantum theory

——————— SOME FOOTBALL MASCOTS OF NOTE ———————

Arsenal	*Gunnersaurus Rex*		Leicester City	*Filbert Fox*
Aston Villa	*Hercules Lion*		Manchester City	*Moonchester*
Birmingham City	*Beau Brummie*		Manchester Utd	*Fred the Red*
Blackburn Rovers	*Roar Lion*		Middlesbrough	*Roary Lion*
Bradford City	*Billy Bantam*		Millwall	*Zampa the Lion*
Cardiff	*Bartley the Bluebird*		Newcastle Utd	*Monty Magpie*
Charlton	*Floyd & Harvey*		Norwich City	*Captain Canary*
Chelsea	*Stamford Lion*		Oldham	*Chaddy the Owl*
Colchester Utd	*Eddie the Eagle*		Portsmouth	*Nelson the Dog*
Everton	*Mr Toffee*		Southampton	*Super Saint*
Fulham	*Terry Bytes*		Spurs	*Chirpy Cockerel*
Grimsby	*The Mighty Mariner*		Swansea	*Cyril the Swan‡*
Hartlepool	*H'Angus the Monkey†*		West Ham	*Harry the Hammer*
Ipswich Town	*Bluey the Horse*		Wimbledon	*Wandle the Womble*
Leeds Utd	*Ellie the Elephant*		Wolves	*Wolfie & Wendy*

† In 2002 *H'Angus the Monkey* was elected Mayor of Hartlepool, on the manifesto of free bananas for kids. Hartlepool have a monkey as a mascot, as townsfolk were said to have hanged a monkey during the Napoleonic wars as they suspected it of being a French spy.
‡ *Cyril the Swan* was infamously accused of bringing the game into disrepute after attacking *Zampa the Lion* – ripping off his 'head', and drop-kicking it into the crowd.

——————— BOOKMAKER'S WISDOM ———————

If you back favourites, you'll have no laces in your boots.
If you back outsiders, you'll have no boots.

— JOE *'King of the ring'* THOMPSON, bookmaker, *c.*1860

HAT-TRICKS

In sporting terms, the hat-trick was originally a cricketing phrase for the feat of taking three wickets in three successive balls. There is some debate as to the origin of the term – some claiming that the bowler was given a new hat by the members of his team[†]; others claiming that the bowler's hat was used as the receptacle for an informal whip-round. Either way, since the C19th the term has escaped the boundaries of the cricket pitch, and is generally used for any kind of triplet in any sporting endeavour.

[†] In 1858 D.V.P. Wright actually was presented with a new hat having bowled a hat-trick.

FOLDING 'THE BANDIT'

HOT BATHS, BATHING, & EUREKA!

Few things are more conducive to idleness than a hot bath and – Archimedes aside[†] – the bathtub can rightly be viewed as offering some respite from the exertions of everyday life. It is no mistake that victorious gladiators would repair to the baths of imperial Rome, or that sports physios sometimes recommend hot baths for post-match warm-downs. The following classification of bathing-water temperatures is from the 1904 edition of B. Bradshaw's *Bathing Places and Climatic Health Resorts*:

Cold	40–50°F	Warm	90
Cool	60	Hot	100–103
Tepid	70–80	Hot as can be borne	115–125

'Hot baths, if continued for any length of time, are very enervating and should usually be followed by a cool sponging of the surface.'

[†] Syracusan mathematician Archimedes (*c.*287–212BC) was commissioned by King Hiero II to test the purity of a gold votive crown which the King suspected had been forged with inferior metals. Archimedes, observing while getting into his bath that some of the bathwater overflowed, quickly realised that an object floating in a liquid displaces a weight of liquid equal to its own weight. Since silver is less dense than gold, 1lb of silver is bulkier than a 1lb of gold and will displace more water. Thus Archimedes was able to prove that Hiero's crown was impure. This observation was famously accompanied by the exclamation *Eureka!* – the Greek for 'I have found it!'.

LEG BYE WIDE DEAD BALL

LAST HOUR OUT! NO BALL

SIX BYE FOUR

—CRICKET UMPIRING SIGNALS · DICKIE BIRD—

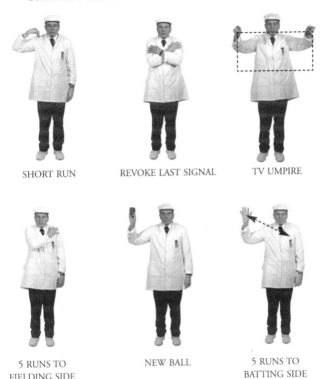

SHORT RUN   REVOKE LAST SIGNAL   TV UMPIRE

5 RUNS TO   NEW BALL   5 RUNS TO
FIELDING SIDE   BATTING SIDE

Harold 'Dickie' Bird MBE is almost certainly the most famous cricket umpire to have taken stand behind the wicket. Having played county cricket for Yorkshire and Leicestershire (his highest first-class score was 181 not out *vs* Glamorgan) Dickie took up umpiring in 1966. In a career spanning 32 years he presided over 68 test matches and 92 one-day internationals, and was the first man to have umpired 3 World Cup finals.

—MOTTO OF THE ROYAL LIFE SAVING SOCIETY—

QUEMCUNQUE MISERUM VIDERIS HOMINEM SCIAS
whosoever you see in distress, recognise in him a fellow man

MONOPOLY MONEY

At the beginning of every game of Monopoly each player receives
£1,500 from the Bank in the following denominations:

$2 \times £500 \cdot 4 \times £100 \cdot 1 \times £50 \cdot 1 \times £20 \cdot 2 \times £10 \cdot 1 \times £5 \cdot 5 \times £1$

DISCONTINUED & DEMONSTRATION OLYMPIC SPORTS

A number of sports have been included at Olympic Games of the past as
demonstration sports not eligible for medals – a practice which has been
discontinued since 1992. In addition, a number of sports have fallen out
of favour and are no longer part of the modern Olympic roll-call. The list
below tabulates these sports, along with the last year of their inclusion:

DEMONSTRATION SPORTS		DISCONTINUED SPORTS	
American football	1932	Cricket	1900
Australian rules football	1956	Croquet‡	1900
Bandy	1952	Golf	1904
Bicycle polo†	1908	Jeu de paume	1908
Budo	1964	Lacrosse	1908
Dog sled racing	1932	Motor boating	1908
Gliding	1936	Polo	1936
Jeu de paume	1928	Racquets	1908
Korfball	1928	Roque	1904
Lacrosse	1948	Rugby union	1924
Military patrol	1948	Tug of war	1920
Pelota basque	1992		
Roller hockey	1992	
Speed skiing	1992	
Water skiing	1972	
Winter pentathlon	1948	

† *The one and only Olympic bicycle polo match was played between Germany and the Irish Bicycle Polo Association.*
‡ *All contestants in the event were French.*

Only 5 sports have been contested at every modern Olympics since 1896:

ATHLETICS · CYCLING · FENCING · GYMNASTICS · SWIMMING

For the IOC to recognise a sport (though this does not guarantee it will
be contested at a Games) it must meet the following minimum criteria:

Men's sport .... *widely played in at least 75 countries on 4 continents*
Women's sport .... *widely played in at least 40 countries on 3 continents*
Winter sport .... *widely played in at least 25 countries on 3 continents*

——— LONDON BRIDGE-HAND NICKNAMES ———

A range of terms is employed by some of the more informal bridge players in London to describe a hand with a preponderance of a particular suit:

DIAMONDS........	*Hatton Garden*	HEARTS[†]	*The Brompton*
CLUBS	*St James's*	SPADES	*Kew Gardens*

† Named after the Brompton Hospital – a specialist cardiac hospital in West London. This hospital is probably also the source of the (in)famous Brompton Cocktail: a mixture of morphine (or heroin), cocaine, alcohol, chloroform, water, and flavouring, which was on occasion prescribed to those suffering from the intractable pain of terminal illness.

——————— SOLVING MARBLE SOLITAIRE ———————

Listed here are the moves required to solve a standard thirty-two piece game of marble solitaire – should all else have failed.

Move		to		take					
d2	⇒	d4	∴	d3	c7	⇒	c5	∴	c6
f3	⇒	d3	∴	e3	c2	⇒	c4	∴	c3
e1	⇒	e3	∴	e2	a3	⇒	c3	∴	b3
e4	⇒	e2	∴	e3	d3	⇒	b3	∴	c3
c1	⇒	e1	∴	d1	a5	⇒	a3	∴	a4
e1	⇒	e3	∴	e2	a3	⇒	c3	∴	b3
e6	⇒	e4	∴	e5	d5	⇒	d3	∴	d4
g5	⇒	e5	∴	f5	d3	⇒	b3	∴	c3
d5	⇒	f5	∴	e5	b3	⇒	b5	∴	b4
g3	⇒	g5	∴	g4	b5	⇒	d5	∴	c5
g5	⇒	e5	∴	f5	d5	⇒	f5	∴	e5
b5	⇒	d5	∴	c5	f4	⇒	d4	∴	e4
c7	⇒	c5	∴	c6	c4	⇒	e4	∴	d4
c4	⇒	c6	∴	c5	e3	⇒	e5	∴	e4
e7	⇒	c7	∴	d7	f5	⇒	d5	∴	e5
					d6	⇒	d4	∴	d5

Solitaire is, as its name implies, a game for a solitary player; and it has the great merit that it can be played with equal enjoyment and profit by children, by invalids, and – in their spare moments – by Professors of Higher Mathematics.

— EDMOND HOYLE (1672–1769)

——————— NETBALL POSITION CODES ———————

GS	Goal Shooter	WD................	Wing Defence
GA..................	Goal Attack	GD	Goal Defence
WA................	Wing Attack	GK...................	Goal Keeper
C...........................	Centre	*(Only the GS & GA can score goals)*	

—————————— NAVEL GAZING ——————————

The navel, umbilicus, omphalodium, or belly-button is the round cicatrix (scar-tissue) protuberance located on the abdomen where the umbilical cord was originally attached. Since the dawn of time the navel has been the focus of a reflective form of philosophical contemplation known as Omphalopsychism. This might be because the navel literally represents the location of birth, or perhaps because it is where the eye lazily falls when one is reclining naked. A number of Omphalopsychite groups have existed through history – perhaps the most famous of which were the Hesychasts, a sect of quietists who (from *c.*1050AD) practised gazing at the navel to induce a hypnotic reverie. The Hesychasts believed that through a rigorous regime of ascetisism, devotion, and deep contemplation of the body, a mystic light – no less than the uncreated divine light of God – could be seen. The question of whether Adam and Eve had navels (given that they were created by God) is one which has vexed theologians for some time. Incidentally, a number of artists, not least Albrecht Dürer and William Blake, have chosen to depict Adam and Eve *with* omphalodia.

————— HORSE-RACING WINNING MARGINS —————

The following schematic shows the order of winning margins in racing:

A *length* is the distance from a horse's nose to the start of its tail (roughly 8 feet). In professional racing, margins tend to be measured in time: in flat racing, 1 second = 5 *lengths*; in jump racing, 1 second = 4 *lengths*. A *distance* is usually employed to describe a margin longer than 30 *lengths*.

————————— PARDONING BULLS —————————

In bullfighting an *indulto* is a pardon granted to a bull by the *presidente* of the fight for demonstrating extraordinary braveness. Some of the *toros célebres* (famous bulls) granted the *indulto* include: Algareño, Civilón, Gordito (who killed 21 horses during a fight in 1869), and Jaquéton – whose name is given as a nickname to other bulls considered to be brave.

PAC MAN

The name *Pac Man* derives from the Japanese 'paku paku' – a term that refers to the motion of the mouth as it opens and closes while eating. (The original game was called *Pukman*, though this was swiftly changed for the Western market when it became clear how easily the initial letter could be modified for obscene effect.) The game's principal designer, Toru Iwatani, claims that *Pac Man's* iconic character was inspired when he saw a pan of pizza with a slice removed, and the marriage of maze-based game with cartoon-like food consumption developed from there. To complete a level, *Pac Man* must gobble up the 240 *dots* and 4 *energizers* which fill each maze while being pursued by 4 *ghosts* who will eliminate one of his three lives each time they run into him. *Pac Man* scores bonus points by eating the *fruits* and *prizes* which occasionally appear, and by eating the *ghosts* when they have been rendered temporarily vulnerable (and blue) by the *energizers*. The *ghosts* are known by a variety of names and nicknames:

Japanese name	Japanese nickname		English name	English nickname
Oikake	*Akabei*	RED	Shadow	*Blinky*
Machibuse	*Pinky*	PINK	Speedy	*Pinky*
Kimagure	*Aosuke*	CYAN	Bashful	*Inky*
Otoboke	*Guzuta*	ORANGE	Pokey	*Clyde*

Each ghost has a distinct personality: *Pinky* is nifty, often hovering just in front of *Pac Man's* gobbling mouth; *Blinky* tends to follow in dogged pursuit; *Inky* is bashful, sometimes even fleeing from *Pac Man*; and *Clyde* is just plain slow. Complex algorithms allow the ghosts to team up in group attacks and then disperse – an attempt by the programmers to prevent players from becoming discouraged. The Holy Grail of 'classic' *Pac Man* (which spawned a wealth of spin-off games) is to eat every *dot*, every *energizer*, every blue *ghost*, and every *fruit* and *prize* on all 256 levels without losing a single life[†]. On 3 July 1999, Billy Mitchell became the first to accomplish this feat, playing for six hours on a single quarter.

† Everything *Pac Man* gobbles has a point value: *dots* = 10 points; *energizers* = 50 points; *dark blue ghosts* = 200, 400, 800, and 1600 respectively; *cherries* = 100; *strawberries* = 300; *peaches* = 500; *apples* = 700; *grapes* = 1000; *Galaxians* = 2000; *bells* = 3000; *keys* = 5000. Billy Mitchell's maximum *Pac Man* score, therefore, was an astonishing 3,333,360 points.

PUSH SHOTS

Illegal in snooker but permitted in pool, PUSH SHOTS occur when the tip of the cue is touching the white when the white touches the object ball.

RIGGED DICE

For as long as dice have been used for gaming and gambling they have been fixed *(gaffed)* by dice-cheats *(mittmen)* in a variety of novel ways. *Loaded dice* are those secretly weighted – often with a substance (like mercury) that could be tapped into different places to favour a particular number (hence their nickname *tappers* or *peeties*). A *dead deuce* die is loaded on the 5 so that the 2 rolls more frequently. *Floated dice* work on the same principle but with areas hollowed inside the die to favour a particular roll. (*Floaters* can often be detected when placed in a glass of water.) *Caps, honey dice, slicks* or *rubber balls* have one or more faces which are covered in a non-stick material (or are given a rougher surface) so that they are more likely to adhere to the surface of the table. *Shapes* are any dice that are not perfect cubes – and there are many varieties: *Flats* have one or more sides shaved away; *Bevels* have one or more edges rounded off; *Suckers* have a concave side that is said to stick to the table. Dice with *Edge Work* are serrated, shaved, or cut in a certain way as to influence the roll – but are too unreliable for most cheats, and can easily be spotted by others. *Electric dice* with one metallic face were used with magnetic playing surfaces. Casinos that cheated in this way quickly became known by the punters as *juice joints*.

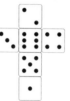

an honest layout

Since *c.*1400BC the opposing sides of six-sided dice have add up to seven in the following manner: 6 faces 1; 5 faces 2; 4 faces 3. Consequently, the most unsubtle of all *gaffed* die are those that are simply misspotted in some way.

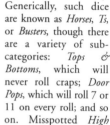

Generically, such dice are known as *Horses, Ts,* or *Busters,* though there are a variety of sub-categories: *Tops & Bottoms,* which will never roll craps; *Door Pops,* which will roll 7 or 11 on every roll; and so on. Misspotted *High Number* and *Low Number* dice are often employed with games like backgammon where high rolls are most useful. When the *mittman* introduces a *gaffed* dice or die into a game (a technique known as *ripping*) those in on the scam can often identify the false die *(brick)* by glancing at the face of the 3 which is often spotted in such a way as to identify it to those in the know. In C16th England rigged dice were known as *Gourds* or *Fulhams* after the louche London suburb notorious for blacklegs and dice cheats. If rigged to throw high numbers (5–12) they were known as *High Fulhams* or *Gourds;* if 1–4 they were known as *Low Fulhams* or *Gourds.* As Shakespeare wrote in *The Merry Wives of Windsor:*

> Let vultures gripe thy guts!
> For gourd and fullam holds
> And 'high' and 'low' beguile
> the rich and poor.

PUB CRICKET

The game of 'pub cricket' was devised to while away the hours of a long and tedious car journey. Each player takes an innings in turn and scores one run for every leg (animal or human) depicted on the pub signs that are passed. Players are 'caught out' if they miss a sign spotted by another player, or 'bowled out' if they pass a sign that has no legs depicted.

Other classic car games include: 'I spy with my little eye'; 'I hear with my little ear'; and 'number-plate poker' where the characters on number-plates are used to form the best poker hand. (The game of Pulpit Cricket is based upon detecting the verbal tics of preachers, scoring a 6, for example, for 'in a very real way'.) Some like to spot Eddie Stobart trucks on the motorway. However, true aficionados eschew this idle pastime, preferring to keep an eye peeled for those vehicles carrying the red and white livery of the European haulier Norbert Dentressangle.

GREYHOUND TRAP COLOUR CODING

	Red	Pink	White	Black	Orange	Black & White	Yellow	Blue	Green	Green & White	Yellow & Black
Great Britain	1		3	4	5		6		2		
Australia	1	8	3	7			2	5	4	6	
Ireland	1		3	4	5		6		2		
USA	1		3	5				6	2	4	7	8
Spain	1		3	4	5		6		2		

TUGS OF WAR ROPE SPECIFICATION

As defined by The Tug of War International Federation:
The rope must not be less than 10 centimetres (100 mm), or more than 12·5 centimetres (125 mm) in circumference, and must be free from knots or other holdings for the hands. The ends of the rope shall have a whipping finish. The minimum length of the rope must not be less than 33·5 metres.

AVERAGE WEIGHT OF GAME, &c.

Blackcock . 3¼–3½lb	Hare......... 6½–7lb	Ptarmigan ... 1–1½lb
Capercailzie.... 6–7lb	Jack Snipe... 1½–2oz	Quail.......... 3½oz
Snipe.......... 2–3oz	Lapwing....... 4–5oz	Rabbit....... 2½–3lb
Golden plover. 4–5oz	Partridge.... 13–14oz	Widgeon . 1½–1¾lb
Grouse....... 1½–2lb	Pheasant..... 2½–3lb	Wild duck... 2–2½lb

THE SOCIAL HIERARCHY OF FALCONRY

Falconry was one of the oldest activities to be called the Sport of Kings (see p.140) – and from its introduction into Britain (see p.12) the sport has been tightly woven into the fabric of the country's class hierarchy. In her idiosyncratic 1486 *Book of St Albans*, Dame Juliana Berners presents a hierarchy of hawks and the social ranks with which they were appropriate:

The EAGLE, VULTURE, or MERLOUN for an EMPEROR

The GER-FALCON for a KING

The FALCON GENTLE for a PRINCE

The FALCON OF THE ROCK for a DUKE

The FALCON PEREGRINE for an EARL

The BUSTARD for a BARON

The SACRE for a KNIGHT

The LANER for an ESQUIRE

The MARYLON for a LADY

The HOBBY for a young MAN

The GOS-HAWK for a YEOMAN

The TERCEL for a POOR MAN

The SPARROW-HAWK for a PRIEST

The MUSKET for a HOLY WATER CLERK

The KESTREL for a KNAVE

THE FOOTBALL LEAGUE TWELVE

Below are the original twelve teams of the Football League, which was founded in 1888 at the instigation of William McGregor (of Aston Villa):

Accrington FC... *(established)*	1878	Everton	1878
Aston Villa	1874	Notts County	1862
Blackburn Rovers	1875	Preston North End	1881
Bolton Wanderers	1874	Stoke	1863
Burnley	1882	West Bromwich Albion	1878
Derby County	1884	Wolverhampton Wanderers	1877

THE IMMORTAL GAME

Played between two mathematics teachers, Adolf Anderssen and Lionel Kieseritzky, at the Chess Divan at Simpson's-in-the-Strand in 1851, the 'Immortal' Game has become one of the most famous battles of chess (even though some question the merit of this fame). In his day Anderssen was considered to be one of the world's strongest tournament players and his daring sacrifice of a bishop, two rooks, and his queen to force checkmate was seen as both creative and bold. Wilhelm Steinitz declared: 'in this game there occurs almost a continuity of brilliancies, every one of which bears the stamp of intuitive genius, that could have been little assisted by calculations, as the combination-point arises only at the very end of the game.' Ernst Falkbeer gave the match its nickname in 1855, though actual immortality has been guaranteed in a number of ways. In 1984 Surinam issued a 90c stamp with a layout of the board after the 20th move; a version of the endgame is played between Sebastian and Tyrell in Ridley Scott's 1982 film *Blade Runner*; and since 1923 the townsfolk of Marostica in Italy have played out the game on a life-size board with real human players.

Anderssen [white] · **Kieseritzky** [black]

1	...e4	e5	13	..h5...Qg5
2	..f4	exf4	14	..Qf3.....Ng8
3	...Bc4	..Qh4+	15	..Bxf4....Qf6
4	..Kf1	b5	16	..Nc3.....Na6
5	..Bxb5	...Nf6	17	..Nd5...Qxb2
6	..Nf3	....Qh6	18	..Bd6...Bxg1
7	..d3	....Nh5	19	..e5...Qxa1+
8	..Nh4	....Qg5	20	..Ke2....Na6
9	..Nf5	...c6	21	..Nxg7+..Kd8
10	..g4	....Nf6	22	..Qf6+...Nxf6
11	..Rg1	....cxb5	23	..Be7#....1-0
12	..h4	....Qg6	*See p.80 for notation.*

Curiously, sources differ in their account of the moves, and some assert that Kieseritzky actually resigned after the 20th move. The diagram below shows the final state of the board after Anderssen achieved mate in the 23rd move:

IDLE WORMS

It used to be said that little worms ('idle worms') bred in the fingers of indolent servants, to which Shakespeare alludes in *Romeo & Juliet* [I. iv.]:

'A round little worm Pricked from the lazy finger of a maid'

CHEATING & GAMESMANSHIP

TONYA HARDING plotted to have her rival Nancy Kerrigan nobbled by an assailant before the 1994 US National Skating Championships.

ROSIE RUIZ was the first woman to finish the Boston Marathon in 1980 – after joining the race just half a mile from the end. (Ruiz had only qualified for the Boston race after a fast time in New York when she had taken the subway.) Ruiz may have been inspired by FRED LORZ, who won the 1904 St Louis Olympics marathon by 'running' 11 miles as a passenger in a car.

THE SPANISH INTELLECTUALLY DISABLED BASKETBALL TEAM won paralympic Gold in 2000. However, it transpired that 10 of the 12 team members had no intellectual disability whatsoever.

An age-old scam of golf cheats is 'inch creeping', where players edge their balls nearer to the hole when they mark them on the green. In 1985, a Scottish professional was banned from playing as a pro for 20 years by the PGA for 'inch creeping' his ball up to 20 feet.

In the Tintin adventure *Flight 714* the millionaire who never laughs, LASZLO CARREIDAS, cheats at a game of battleships with Captain Haddock. Carreidas uses CCTV aboard his private jet to spy on the Captain's board – however, he gets his comeuppance as the aeroplane is hijacked and Carreidas never gets to finish the game.

WILLIAM WEBB ELLIS, a pupil of Rugby school, is usually (if almost certainly erroneously†) credited with creating the game of rugby in 1832 when, cheating during a game of football, he picked up the ball and ran with it. The school commemorates this act, calling it 'fine disregard for the rules'. However, young William was described by a contemporary as 'one who was inclined to take unfair advantages at football'.

†Considerable doubt surrounds this story, not least because it seems never to have been told by Webb Ellis himself. Instead, it was recounted by an old Rugbeian, Matthew Holbeche Bloxam, some fifty years after the event. Notwithstanding this, many similar games existed prior to William's cheating, including *Harpastum* – a Roman game that involved both scrummaging and the carrying of the ball.

AURIC GOLDFINGER, villain of the eponymous Bond film, cheats not only at cards (see p.18), but also at golf. James Bond outfoxes him both times – on the golf-course switching Goldfinger's Slazenger 1 for a Slazenger 7: '...we are playing by strict rules so I'm afraid you lose the hole and the match.'

STELLA WALSH set twenty world records, won Gold in the 100m in the 1932 Olympics, and was inducted into the US Track and Field Hall of Fame. However, an autopsy after her murder revealed that Walsh suffered from the rare genetic disease Mosaicism, which endowed 'her' with male genitals and chromosomes of both sexes.

———— CHEATING & GAMESMANSHIP cont. ————

During the Ashes tour of 1932–3 the England captain Douglas Jardine employed the controversial BODYLINE bowling technique (known also as 'leg theory') in an attempt to contain the devastating talent of Australian batsman Don Bradman. Pace bowlers such as Harold Larwood and Bill Voce were instructed to pitch short, fast balls directly at the batsman's body – a tactic that left the Australians the unenviable choice of being hit by the ball or risking an easy catch to the phalanx of fielders Jardine had placed short on the leg side. While England's tactics fell short of actual cheating, they were condemned by many as the nadir of unsporting play. Australia's captain Bill Woodfull said 'there are two teams out there. One is trying to play cricket'. In contrast, when Larwood's fast bowling felled Woodfull with a blow to the heart, Captain Jardine quipped, 'Well bowled, Harold!' In response to 'leg theory' the rules of cricket were changed to limit the number of fielders behind square leg.

DIEGO MARADONA blatantly scored a 52nd-minute goal against England in the 1986 World Cup with his hand. He later claimed: 'It was partly the hand of Maradona and partly the hand of God'.

BORIS ONISCHENKO, fencing in the 1976 Olympics in Montreal, wired up his épée so that he could trigger the electronic scoring system at will.

In the 1970s & 1980s EAST GERMANY suddenly began to rival the USA & USSR in the medals stakes. It emerged that in their desperation to prove Eastern superiority, the state had sponsored drug taking, telling the athletes they were vitamins.

During the 1978 *Tour de France*, cyclist MICHEL POLLENTIER used a system of rubber tubing to provide a fake urine sample. This foreshadowed Danny's invention of 'a device enabling the drunken driver to operate in absolute safety' described in the film *Withnail & I*. The 1998 *Tour de France* was dubbed the *Tour de Dopage*, after 234 doses of the drug EPO were found in a Festina team's car.

Eight members of the CHICAGO WHITESOX baseball team were charged with 'throwing' the 1919 World Series in return for huge bribes from a gang of gamblers. A number of players confessed, including 'Shoeless' Joe Jackson, and all eight were suspended.

In 1981, when Australia were playing New Zealand in a World Series Cup game at the MCG, New Zealand required six off the final ball to win the match. In an act of supreme gamesmanship, the Aussie captain GREG CHAPPELL instructed his brother Trevor to bowl an underarm 'grubber' along the grass, making it impossible for the New Zealand number ten, Brian McKechnie, to hit a six.

FENCING BLADES & THEIR TARGETS

The FOIL is the modern version of a sword designed to aid duelling practice. It is the lightest of the three weapons. The target area is the torso (both front and back), excluding the head. Valid hits can only be scored with the point of the blade.

The ÉPÉE is the modern version of the duelling rapier, and is the heaviest of the three weapons. The target area is the whole body, and whoever hits first scores a point (if both fighters should make a hit at the same time, both score a point).

The SABRE is the modern version of the cavalry sword, and is designed as a cutting weapon. The target area mirrors that of a horseman, and is anywhere above the waist, including head and arms. Hits are scored with the point or the cutting edges.

weight <500g
blade length 90cm

weight <770g
blade length 90cm

weight <500g
blade length 88cm

SCORING BILLIARDS

Cannon	2	Pot red	3
Pot white	2	In-off red	3
In-off white	2	*If combined in a stroke, all are scored*	

In-offs hit with a cannon score, in addition to the cannon, the following:

If the red was struck first by the cue-ball 3
If the object white was struck first 2
If both object balls were struck simultaneously 2

GAMBLING CRUSADERS

In 1190, Kings Richard I and Philip of France jointly established an edict regulating gambling with games of chance by members of the Christian crusading armies. No person under the rank of KNIGHT was permitted to play any game for money; KNIGHTS and CLERGYMEN could play for stakes lower than 20 shillings per day and night; the MONARCHS could, naturally, play for whatever stakes they chose, but their attendants were restricted to stakes of 20 shillings. If any exceeded this sum, they were to be whipped, naked, through the ranks of the troops for three whole days.

SOME COLLECTORS & THEIR COLLECTIONS

Collector	Collects
antiquist	antiques
arctophile	teddy-bears
bibliophile	books
broadsider	broadsides
chiffonier	scraps of fabric
conchologist	shells
copoclephile	key-rings
crabologist	crabs
deltiologist	postcards
discophile	gramophone records
incunabulist	early books
logophile	words
notaphilic	banknotes
numismatist	coins
pasquinader	lampoons, satires
philatelist	stamps
phillumenist	matchbooks
preterist	historical objects
rhapsodist	literary pieces
tatterer	refuse, rags
tegestologist	beer-mats

PALL MALL

The game 'Pall Mall' (also Pell Mell, Palle-malle, Paille Maille, Pelemele, or Jeu de Mail) originated in Italy during the C16th. It was introduced to England, via France, around the time of Charles I's coronation, and it was swiftly adopted by the aristocracy. The first royal Pall Mall alley was built inside St James's Park, but clouds of dust thrown up by carriages on their journeys to and from the Palace and Charing Cross began to obscure the balls. Consequently, in 1661 a new alley was constructed between two rows of elms just north of the first site. Originally named Catherine Street (in honour of Catherine of Braganza), the alley was known as Pall Mall – a colloquialism that remains to this day. The game itself was a kind of golf that involved striking a boxwood ball along an alley (*c.*800yds) with a mallet, then hooking it up with a spoon-like gaff through an iron ring suspended above the ground. The player who succeeded in getting the ball through the ring in the fewest strokes (or within an agreed number of strokes) was declared the winner. Samuel Pepys first witnessed Pelemele on 2 April 1661 when he came across a game played by the Duke of York.

OLYMPIC DISCUS SPECIFICATIONS

♂ weight 2kg; diameter 219–21mm · ♀ weight 1kg; diameter 180–2mm

CLASSIFICATION OF 'BLIND' SPORTSMEN

In an attempt to prevent cheating and to ensure fair competition, disabled and impaired sporting organisations employ medical tests to assess the degree of impairment of sportsmen and women. For example, by measuring an athlete's best eye at its highest possible correction, the International Blind Sports Federation (IBSF) classifies the blind and visually impaired into the following four groups:

[NOE] · Not eligible; a visual acuity over 6/60 and/or visual field of more than 20 degrees.

[B3] · From a visual acuity of above 2/60 to a visual acuity of 6/60 and/or a visual field or more than 5 degrees and less than 20 degrees.

[B2] · From the ability to recognise the form of a hand to a visual acuity of 2/60 and/or a visual field of less than 5 degrees.

[B1] · Total absence of perception of the light in both eyes, or some perception of the light but with inability to recognise the form of a hand at any distance and in any direction.

SLEDGING IN CRICKET

As in all competitive sports, verbal intimidation and abuse have long been a feature of cricket (see W.G. Grace p.73). Yet it seems that in the 1970s this tactic became increasingly aggressive (and, some claim, organised) in the form of 'sledging' – where bowlers and fielders maintain a barrage of sometimes breathtakingly vituperative and obscene invective against the opposition batsmen. (The term is said to derive from 'sledgehammer' – an indication of the subtlety of the abuse as well as its intended effect.) Although Australia is the side most commonly associated with sledging, verbal abuse is by no means restricted to that country, and a host of players have talked obliquely about 'mental disintegration' as an element of their team's strategy. That said, Merv Hughes claimed 'if he's mentally weak and I don't try to put pressure on that side of his game, then I'm not doing my job'. And, commenting on such verbal assaults, Australian PM Bob Hawke claimed 'I don't think our boys have played unfairly, they've not cheated, but they push things reasonably hard on the pressure'. In contrast Mike Brearley denounced sledging as 'a totally unwelcome aberration in the game, inane, humourless, and unacceptable'. Geoff Boycott apparently once claimed 'they use words I've never heard before'.

❧ In the traditional slang of barristers to 'go into the ROPE-WALK' was to take up a criminal practice at the Old Bailey – 'ropes' was a nickname for ne'er-do-wells, footpads, ruffians, vagabonds, and the like. ❧ To WALK AT ROVER'S is to wander aimlessly with no fixed abode. ❧ The notion of the WALKING WOUNDED (i.e. prisoners who could make their own way to the medics) originated during the horrors of WWI. ❧ To WALK THE CHALK is a military and police term for pacing along a chalked line to demonstrate one's (in)sobriety. WALK YOUR CHALK! was an instruction to quit one's lodgings – it might originate from the practice of chalking the doors of houses that were to be requisitioned by the army or monarchy. ❧ SLEEPWALKING (also noctambulation or somnambulism) tends to occur in the deep stages of NREM sleep (see p.88) and tends to last from a few minutes to half-an-hour. During episodes of sleepwalking, individuals are usually able to perform complex motor functions and often have no memory of their actions when they awake. ❧ As *Dire Straits* noted: 'And after all the violence and double talk, There's just a song in all the trouble and the strife, You do the walk, you do the WALK OF LIFE.' ❧ When Australian Aboriginals GO WALKABOUT they return to the bush for a time to escape Westernised life. When members of the Royal Family GO WALKABOUT they leave the comfort of their cars to shake hands with the *hoi polloi*. ❧ A baseball hitter gets a WALK to 1st base if he is pitched four 'balls' or is touched by a pitched ball. ❧ DOBBY'S WALK is the area haunted by a goblin – in the C19th a 'dobbie' was a household sprite or apparition. ❧ When batsmen WALK in cricket, they abandon the crease even before the umpire has given them out (see p.90). As Brian Close said: 'A batsman who knows he is out should walk. That is the way we play the game.' ❧ The LAMBETH WALK is a road in South London which was featured in the 1937 musical *Me and My Gal*. The song (*'Any time you're Lambeth way, Any evening, any day, You'll find us all, Doin' the Lambeth walk'*) was accompanied by a strutting, thumb-jerking dance, and the occasional ejaculation of *'Oi!'*. ❧ A C19th dance of African-American origin, the CAKEWALK originated when slaves parodied the 'genteel' manners of their owners. Dancers would promenade the dancefloor, improvising moves, and the most stylish would be awarded a cake. ❧ The Minister of SILLY WALKS (John Cleese) was not at all impressed with Mr Pudey's (Michael Palin's) silly walk: 'It's not particularly silly, is it? I mean, the right leg isn't silly at all and the left leg merely does a forward aerial half turn every alternate step.' ❧ To GO BY WALKER'S BUS, to TAKE THE MARROWBONE STAGE, and to RIDE SHANK'S PONY are all euphemisms for walking. ❧ In shooting parlance, beaters drive or WALK UP to dislodge birds from the undergrowth into the oncoming hail of shot. ❧ To be ordered to WALK SPANISH is to be made redundant, as is to be given one's MARCHING ORDERS or WALKING PAPERS. ❧ [See also p.21 & p.143.] ❧

———————— ON FITNESS & EXERCISE ————————

MARK TWAIN · I have never taken any exercise except sleeping and resting, and I never intend to take any. Exercise is loathsome. And it cannot be any benefit when you are tired; and I was always tired.

ROBERT MAYNARD HUTCHINS · Whenever the urge to exercise comes upon me, I lie down for a while and it passes.

NEIL ARMSTRONG [attrib.] · I believe that every human has a finite number of heart-beats. I don't intend to waste any of mine running around doing exercises.

BARBARA EHRENREICH · Exercise is the yuppie version of bulimia.

HENRY FORD · Exercise is bunk – if you are healthy, you don't need it. If you are sick, you shouldn't take it.

ANNA QUINDLEN · I feel about exercise the same way that I feel about a few other things: that there is nothing wrong with it if it is done in private by consenting adults.

JOHN F. KENNEDY · Our growing softness, our increasing lack of physical fitness, is a menace to our security.

BARRY GRAY · I get my exercise running to the funerals of my friends who exercise.

———————— CALORIE EXPENDITURE ————————

The approximate Calories burnt each minute by those weighing *c.*150lb:

Sitting still 1–2	Yoga 4–6	Skipping 7–9
Snooker 2–6	Dancing 4–6	Tennis 7–9
Walking 2–6	Skipping 4–7	Morris dancing . 7–10
Frisbee 3–5	Badminton 5–6	Tennis 7–12
Fishing 3–6	Brisk walking 5–8	Football 7–13
Housework 3–6	Aerobics class 5–9	Basketball 8–11
Golf 3–6	Ping-pong 6–7	Jogging 8–13
Cricket 3–7	Water skiing 6–9	Langlauf 8–13
Trampoline 3–9	Sex 6–11	Martial arts 8–13
Fencing 4–6	Swimming 6–12	Squash 8–13
Gymnastics 4–6	Ice skating 7–9	Water-polo 8–13

These figures are approximate and will vary depending on a number of factors, from how vigorous the gymnastics, to the incline of the hill climbed, or the weight of the golf clubs carried. For every pound over 150lb, add 10%; for every pound under 150lb, subtract 10%. With a small 'c', a calorie is the amount of energy required to heat 1g of water by 1°C. With a capital 'C' (a kilocalorie or 1,000 calories) it is the amount of energy required to heat 1kg of water by 1°C, or 4.2kJ. [Sadly, 1 chocolate éclair = *c.*190 Calories.]

CURLING

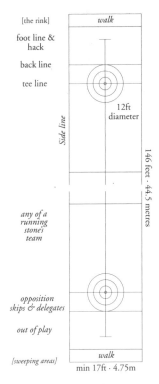

[the rink]
walk
foot line & hack
back line
tee line
12ft diameter
Side line
146 feet · 44.5 metres
any of a running stone's team
opposition skips & delegates
out of play
[sweeping areas]
walk
min 17ft · 4.75m

Curling originated in Scotland, where it was played on frozen ponds. Like an icy version of bowls, two teams of four compete in the best of eight 'ends'. The object of each end is to place as many stones within the scoring area, using strategy to try and ensure your team scores the most, whilst expelling or blocking your opponents' stones from the 'house'. Curling's most conspicuous quirk is the use of brooms to sweep before the curling stones. This splendidly domestic activity serves to stop the stones bending and speeds their flight.

SOME CURLING TERMS

Rink . . . . *a curling team*
Skip . . . . *captain of the team*
House . . . . *name of the scoring area*
Eight-ender . . . . . . *a perfect end when every stone scores a point*
End . . . . *a round*
Bonspiel . . . . *a curling tournament*
Button . . . . *the centre of the target*
Gripper . . . . *ridged curling shoe*
Slider . . . . *smooth curling shoe*
Hurry . . . . *encouragement to sweepers*

A curling team consists of four players who throw two stones (or rocks) in turn – alternating with the opposition players. The other players on the team act as sweepers. The *lead* throws the 1st & 2nd stones, setting up play, and then sweeps for the next 6. The *second* throws the 3rd & 4th, aiming to take out the other team's stones. The *third* (also known as *vice* or *mate*), throws the 5th & 6th rocks, aiming to set the stage for the *skip* or *captain*, who throws remaining stones which often prove to be vital.

Shot number	who throws	who sweeps
1 & 2	Lead	Second & Third
3 & 4	Second	Lead & Third
5 & 6	Third	Lead & Second
7 & 8	Skip	Lead & Second

SATCHEL'S ADVICE

The legendary baseball pitcher Leroy 'Satchel' Paige (1906?–82) was famed as much for his fast wit as his fast balls. He played in over 2,500 games and notched up more than 50 no-hitters. In 1948 Paige was the first black pitcher in the American League, and in 1971 he made history as the first 'Negro League' player to be inducted into the Baseball Hall of Fame. He printed the following advice to fans on the back of his autograph cards:

'Six Rules For A Happy Life'
Avoid fried meats which angry up the blood.
If your stomach disputes you, lie down and pacify it with cool thoughts.
Keep the juices flowing by jangling around gently as you move.
Go very lightly on vices such as carrying on
in society. The social ramble ain't restful.
Avoid running at all times.
Don't look back. Something may be gaining on you.

REGAL SPORTS & LOVE

I know how to perform eight exercises: I fight with courage; I keep a firm seat on horseback; I am skilled in swimming; I glide along the ice on skates; I excel in darting the lance; I am dexterous at the oar; and yet a Russian maid disdains me.

— HAROLD II (1022–66) [attrib.]

ROCK, PAPER, SCISSORS

The origin of the classic game of ROCK, PAPER, SCISSORS has been the subject of much debate. It is possible that a version of the game may have been played by Roman soldiers, who used WATER, FIRE, WOOD (water extinguishes fire, which burns wood, which floats on water). However, no record of the hand signals has been discovered. The Japanese call the game *Jan-ken-poh* or *Janken* – and they use it as a method to choose the dealer in card games, who will serve first at tennis, and so on. (*Hasami* is scissors; *kami* is paper; *ishi* is stone.) Some versions of the game employ four possible hand shapes. For example, French schoolchildren nowadays play with ROCK *(caillou)*, WELL *(puits)*, PAPER *(feuille)*, and SCISSORS *(sciseaux)*. Here, scissors fall down the well, which is covered by paper, which is cut by scissors, which are smashed by rock, which also falls down the well. And, there is an ancient Abyssinian variation with eight signs: needle, sword, scissors, hammer, Imperial razor, sea, altar, and the sky.

—— BACKGAMMON BOARD LAYOUT & TERMS ——

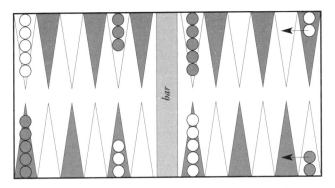

Backgammon	a game won when the loser has *borne off* no *men* and still has *men* on the *bar* or in the winner's *home board*
Bearing off	removing *men* from the board
Blank	an unplayable roll of the dice
Blot	a *point* occupied by a single *man* vulnerable to a *hit*
Comeback	when a *man* on the *bar* enters and *hits* a *blot*
Crossover	a move across the *bar*
Doublet	a throw of doubles
Enter	to move a *man* off the *bar*
Gammon	a game won when the loser has *borne off* no *men*
Hit	an attack on a *blot*, sending the man to the *bar*
Home table	the side of the board in which the game ends
Making a point	placing two or more *men* on a *point*
Man	a piece
Outer table	the opposite half to the *home table*
Point	one of the 24 triangles
Taking up	removing a *man* from a *blot*
Turn the cube	to offer a double (see below)

When backgammon is played for money, the *doubling cube* may be used to increase the stakes. At any stage before a player has rolled the dice to start a turn, their opponent may offer to continue the game at double the initial stakes – assuming that no double has previously been proposed. If the player accepts (*takes*) the wager the stakes are increased and that player *owns* the *doubling cube* and enjoys the option to propose future doubles. (The *ownership* of the cube alternates depending on who has accepted the last double.) If a player declines (*drops* or *passes*) a double they concede the game and the stakes. The cube itself is marked 2, 4, 8, 16, 32, and 64, and is placed on the *bar* to show the current betting level.

—— TEN-PIN BOWLING SPLITS & TERMS ——

A SPLIT is the combination of pins left standing after the first throw, assuming the first throw has knocked over at least one pin[†] but not all of them (which is known as a STRIKE). A range of terms exists to describe the various possible SPLITS, which vary in difficulty depending on the amount of space between the remaining pins. (SPLITS are called in numerical order.)

Nickname of split	*pins standing after first ball*
BABY *or* MURPHY	2/7 *or* 3/10
BACK ROW	7/8/9/10
BED POSTS *or* GOAL POSTS *or* SNAKE EYES	7/10
BIG FOUR *or* DOUBLE PINOCHLE	4/6/7/10
BIG THREE	1/2/3
BUCKET	2/4/5/8 *or* 3/5/6/9
CHRISTMAS TREE *or* FAITH, HOPE, CHARITY	3/7/10 *or* 2/7/10
CINCINNATI	8/10
CLOTHESLINE *or* PICKET FENCE *or* RAIL	1/2/4/7 *or* 1/3/6/10
DIME STORE	5/10
POISON IVY	3/6/10
SLEEPERS	2/8 *or* 3/9
SOUR APPLE *or* LILLY	5/7/10
STRIKE SPLIT	8/10 *or* 7/9

[†] If the first ball leaves the headpin standing, the remaining balls cannot be termed a split. So, the combinations 1/2/10, 1/2/4/10, 1/3/7, 1/3/6/7, &c. are called WASHOUTS.

In addition to these split nicknames, bowling has a wealth of other terms:

Anchor	*last man on a team to roll*	Moat	*slang for the gutter*
Balsa	*weak strike on the head pin*	Mother in law	*the 7 pin*
Bicycle	*a pin hidden by another*	Nose	*hitting the headpin full on*
Box	*a single frame*	Nothing	*a no-score ball*
Cherry	*taking the front pins*	Open	*frame with no strike or spare*
Creeper	*a slow ball*	Pie alley	*a forgiving lane*
Dodo	*an illegal ball*	Pinching	*over-gripping the ball*
Double	*2 strikes in a row*	Pocket	*space between 1/3 or 1/2*
Five bagger	*5 strikes in a row*	Poodle	*a gutter ball*
Foundation	*a 9th-frame strike*	Sixpack	*6 strikes in a row*
Four bagger	*4 strikes in a row*	Sleeper	*a hidden rear pin*
Graveyards	*low-scoring lanes*	Strike out	*3 strikes in 10th frame*
Headpin	[usually] *the 1 pin*	Tandem	*a pin hidden by another*
Honey	*a sweet roll*	Tap	*to leave one pin standing*
Kingpin	[usually] *the 5 pin*	Turkey	*3 strikes in a row*

—— ON THE NUMBERING OF RUGBY SHIRTS ——

Before the rules of rugby were formalised, any number of players would pitch in on either side. In 1836 the number of players in a Rugby Union side was fixed at 20; in 1876 it fell to 15 (after a trial at the 1876 Oxford *vs* Cambridge Varsity match). Rugby League also had 15 players a side, until the number dropped to 13 in 1906. Although the practice of numbering shirts dates back to a New Zealand *vs* Queensland match in 1897, the convention was only adopted in Britain in 1922 when England played Wales. Traditionally, the fullback wore [1]; the front-row forwards wore [8]–[10]; and the back-row [13]–[15]. Nowadays most clubs use the numbering system laid down by the International Rugby Board, which is:

Loose head prop.... 1	Left flanker......... 6	Left wing.......... 11
Hooker.............. 2	Right flanker 7	Left centre 12
Tight head prop.... 3	Number eight 8	Right centre....... 13
Left lock........... 4	Scrum half 9	Right wing........ 14
Right lock......... 5	Flyhalf 10	Fullback........... 15

Replacements and substitutes are numbered from 16 to 22, depending on their positions.

Before the advent of professionalism a number of clubs had idiosyncratic systems of shirt markings. Bath used not to play a number [13]; and West Hartlepool used not to play a number [5], in memory of John Howe who died on the pitch during a match against Morley in 1992. Until recently, Bristol and Leicester were the last two remaining teams to use a system of letters rather than numbers, although their orders were reversed. So, for example, the Bristol fullback was [A], and the Leicester fullback [O]; the Bristol flyhalf [F], and the Leicester flyhalf [J]; and so on across the team.

—— ESCAPE TO VICTORY TEAMSHEET ——

John Huston's film classic *Escape to Victory* (1981) is set in a German prisoner-of-war camp during WWII. A team of Allied footballers hatch an escape plan using a match against the German national side as cover:

Sylvester Stallone†
Paul van Himst · Co Prins · Russell Osman · Michael Caine
Ossie Ardiles · Bobby Moore · John Wark · Soren Linsted
Mike Summerbee · Pélé

† Kevin O'Callaghan was the original Allied goalkeeper. However, they are forced to break his arm in order that Sylvester Stallone's character (who has information vital to their escape) can be released from solitary confinement to play in his place. Despite a decidedly dodgy 'neutral' referee, the plucky Allies secure a 4–4 draw and, with an overexcited French crowd swarming the pitch, our heroes make their escape (to victory).

─────────── FORMULA ONE FLAGS ───────────

Chequered.. *race has finished*
Red .... *race has been stopped for safety reasons*
Blue................ *a faster car is behind and trying to lap a backmarker*
White .... *warns of a slow-moving vehicle (e.g. safety car)*
Red & yellow striped.............. *track slippery (e.g. due to water or oil)*
Yellow .... *danger ahead; overtaking prohibited*
single yellow wave .... *slow down*
double yellow wave......................... *drivers must be prepared to stop*
Orange disc on black (with number)........ *indicates that a car must stop in*
pits immediately because of a mechanical fault
Black & white diagonals (with number)....... *warning for unsportsmanlike*
behaviour (may be followed by a black flag)
Black (with number) .... *driver must stop in pits immediately*
usually to be disqualified for breaking the rules
Green............................. *hazard cleared; cars can race as normal*

─────────── HOPSCOTCH ───────────

Hopscotch is a playground game played all around the world, with a wide variety of different grids and local rules. The most basic version of the game involves players taking it in turns to throw a flat stone into the first box of a grid. They then hop up and down the grid until they retrieve their stone. Players can place their feet where they like on the undivided areas (e.g. 4), but must straddle the divided areas (e.g. 2 & 3). If a player completes a run without standing on a line or stumbling, they can throw their stone to the next square, and repeat the process. (Variations include: kicking the stone from box to box as you hop; claiming and initialling with chalk a personal square that no other player can land on; or completing the board with a stone balanced variously on your head, foot, or hand.) For years it has been claimed that hopscotch dates to Roman times, when centurions would apparently use the game for fitness training as they travelled up and down the roads to and from the capital. Iona and Peter Opie, the authorities on childhood games, pour scorn on this notion, dating hopscotch to the mid-C17th. However, the myth might explain why 'London' is often chalked on the final turning square.

TAROT CARD INTERPRETATIONS

The Tarot pack consists of 78 cards: 22 picture cards of the *major arcana* and 56 suited cards of the *minor arcana* – and it is likely that these two arcana originally formed separate packs. Debate surrounds the oldest known Tarot pack – some claim the 1415 pack belonging to the Duke of Milan, others the 1392 pack made for Charles VI. Even more debate surrounds the origin, symbolism, design, and interpretation of the cards, which have for centuries been used by mystics, soothsayers, fortune tellers, and charlatans. One interpretation of the *major arcana* is below:

Common interpretation	MAJOR ARCANA	Interpretation if reversed
Important decisions needed	FOOL	*problems from reckless actions*
Strength of will and initiative	MAGICIAN	*failure of nerve; hiding from reality*
Influence & insight of wise woman	PAPESS	*risk of emotional instability*
Fertility, motherhood, protection	EMPRESS	*domestic upheaval; male weakness*
Self-control; power; knowledge	EMPEROR	*immaturity; failed ambition*
Good advice; teaching	POPE	*misinformation, poor advice*
Time of choice; intuition	LOVERS	*danger of moral lapse, indecision*
Victory through effort; triumph	CHARIOT	*overbearing influence, ruthlessness*
Agreement through negotiation	JUSTICE	*partisanship, bias, ill judgement*
The need to slowly plan and think	HERMIT	*refusal to heed good advice*
Start of a new cycle; regeneration	WHEEL	*turn for the worse; good cycle ends*
Courage to take a risk	FORTITUDE	*defeat; failure of nerve*
Wisdom; mental agility	HANGED MAN	*materialism; inner struggle*
Major change (often for good)	DEATH	*the element of chance*
Deft handling of circumstances	TEMPERANCE	*progress thwarted by foolishness*
Hidden forces at work	DEVIL	*lust for or abuse of power*
Capricious suffering; disaster	TOWER	*unnecessary suffering*
Insight; widening horizons	STAR	*rigidity of a closed, narrow mind*
Crisis of faith	MOON	*failure of nerve*
Success against the odds	SUN	*misjudgment ending in failure*
Accomplishment; new beginnings	JUDGEMENT	*wasted opportunities; loss; guilt*
Successful completion of matters	WORLD	*stagnation; inertia; no momentum*

It is claimed that these cards correspond to the 22 letters of the Hebrew alphabet, each with complex numerological and Kabbalistic significance. The cards of the *minor arcana* are grouped into four suits: cups, swords, coins, and staves (or wands), which are said to represent clergy, nobility, merchants, and peasants. Each suit consists of number cards from one to ten and four court cards: King, Queen, Knave, and Knight (see pp. 34, 97). Perhaps the most famous fictional Tarot readers are Madam Sosostris who has 'a wicked pack of cards' in T.S. Eliot's 1922 epic *The Wasteland*, and Solitaire (Jayne Seymour) in the Bond film *Live & Let Die* (1973). When James Bond picks out the Fool, Solitaire smirks 'You have found yourself.'

——CURIOUS SPORTING ACTIVITIES OF NOTE——

LA TOMATINA takes place on the last Wednesday of August (the peak of tomato season) in the Spanish village of Buñol. For two hours more than 90,000 pounds of tomatoes are indiscriminately hurled at everything and everyone by 30,000 or so revellers. It seems this annual food-fight began by accident in the 1940s when a friendly meal got out of hand.

Lincolnshire's STAMFORD BULL RUN originated during the reign of King John. On 13 November each year a bull was let loose in the streets and chased by the town's inhabitants with cudgels and sticks. When exhausted to the point of collapse the bull was beaten to death, cooked, and eaten. In 1788 the first attempts to end the Run were made, but only in 1840 did the good people of Stamford finally desist.

EXTREME IRONING, according to its advocates, combines 'the thrills of an extreme outdoor activity with the satisfaction of a well pressed shirt'. The prerequisites are a hot iron, a challenging physical environment (in oncoming traffic, under water, on a mountainside) a bundle of creased clothing, and perhaps a little starch.

The 22-mile MAN *vs* HORSE RACE has been run in Wales since 1979, when Screaming Lord Sutch was the official starter. In June 2004 it was won by a human for the very first time in 2 hours, 5 min, 9 secs.

Each August Bank Holiday Monday the BOG SNORKELLING CHAMPIONSHIPS take place in the Waen Rhydd peat bog on the outskirts of Llanwrtyd Wells, the smallest town in Great Britain. Competitors complete two lengths of a trench 60 yards long by 4 foot wide cut into the dense peat bog. The participants wear snorkels, flippers, and optional wet suits, but are not allowed to employ any conventional swimming strokes. (A similarly odd contest features snorkelling through the peat bog on mountain bikes.)

Britain's annual CHEESE ROLLING contest takes place each May down Cooper's Hill, near Brockworth in the Gloucestershire Cotswolds. A 7–8lb Double Gloucester cheese is released from the top of the hill, and participants scramble down the precipitous bank (which has gradients of 1:2 and 1:1) in a vain attempt to catch it. Four races are held (one for women) and, in each case, the first to the foot of the hill wins the cheese.

The OMAK SUICIDE RACE has been run each August since 1935 in Omak – a picturesque, rural town in Washington, USA. A 120-foot run-in prepares the 20 or so riders and horses for the 210-foot descent (with a gradient of 62º), at the bottom of which flows the Okanogan River. However, as the number of horses injured or killed has increased, so has the vocal opposition to the race.

— CURIOUS SPORTING ACTIVITIES OF NOTE cont. —

BUZKASHI – the Afghan national sport – translates literally as 'goat grabbing', and for good reason. A headless, hoofless, and eviscerated goat carcass (the *boz*) is placed in the centre of a circle, and two opposing teams on horseback attempt to seize it and carry it to the goal area. [The sport featured in John Frankenheimer's 1971 film classic *The Horsemen*, starring Omar Sharif.]

Twice a year on Christmas Day and New Year's Day the men and boys of Kirkwall (on the Mainland of Orkney) play the KIRKWALL BA'. Traditionally, the two teams were formed by accident of birth: those born north of St Magnus Cathedral are *Doonies* (Doon-the-Gates), those born south are *Uppies* (Up-the-Gates). The BA' is a handmade leather ball filled with cork which, on the stroke of 1pm, is tossed into the assembled crowd from the Mercat Cross in front of the Cathedral. Both teams attempt to get the ball and carry it through the streets to their goals: the *Uppies* try to touch the BA' against a wall in the south of the town; the *Doonies* try to get it into the water of the harbour to the north.

The Columbian sport TEJO is akin to the traditional games of deck quoits or horseshoes except that it involves high explosives. Players attempt to toss a ball, disc, or stone into a target area which contains a series of blasting caps *(totes)*. The player who causes most explosions is deemed the winner.

On the second Sunday of August, LA POURCAILHADE takes place in the French town of Trie-sur-Baïse – one of the largest pig-raising areas in Europe. The festival is dedicated to all things porcine, but the highlight is the 'pig squealing competition' where contestants mimic the sounds that pigs make in a variety of real-life scenarios: eating, copulating, giving birth, facing the butcher, and so on.

SPILE TROSHING is an archaic Borsetshire sport, popular in the village of Ambridge. Participants take a wheel from a hay cart, wind a rope round the axle and attach to it the *slug* (a 20lb weight). The *trosher* has to flick the *spile* into the basket or *bower*. If they manage to get the *spile* in on the first rotation it is a *prime* (3 points); if they miss it is a *blind* (no points). [The *spile* is a wooden cone that controls air flow in beer barrels.] (See also p.81.)

Other curious activities of note include: the WORLD GURNING CONTEST held each year as part of the Egremont Crab Apple Fayre in Cumbria; Finland's famous WIFE-CARRYING championship where husbands carry their wives over a 253·5m obstacle course, in order to win their spouse's weight in ale; the Polish WORLD SCREAMING CHAMPIONSHIP held in Goldap; and the WORLD MOSQUITO KILLING CHAMPIONSHIP held in Pelkosenniemi, Finland, where the 1995 record of 21 mosquitoes killed in five minutes still stands.

―――――――― PARLOUR GAME FORFEITS ――――――――

Some forfeits which may be usefully employed with the games on pp.22–3:

COMPLIMENTS · The victim must pay each of the assembled company a heartfelt compliment.

PERFORM THE PARROT · The victim must ask each person 'If I were a parrot, what would you teach me to say?', and then has to repeat what they are instructed. If a woman instructs a man to say 'Who's a pretty boy then?' the man is obliged to kiss her.

ACT THE SULLEN MUTE · The victim must perform whatever tasks they are instructed without speaking, laughing, or smiling.

CONTRADICTION · For a period of time, the victim must perform the opposite of whatever they are instructed by the company.

MAKING A WILL · The victim must apportion one of their belongings to each member of the company (presumably in a manner which is not legally binding).

TRUTH OR DARE · The victim must answer any question with complete candour, or perform a dare (which may be another of the forfeits here listed).

COURTESY · The victim must go around the room and kneel to the most witty, bow to the prettiest, and kiss the one they love best.

MOODY ROOM · The victim must laugh in one corner of the room, sing in another, cry in another and dance in the last.

TEMPERANCE · The victim must abstain from alcohol for a period of time (a most serious forfeit).

AGONY AUNT · The victim must go round the room and proffer a piece of advice to all present.

ANIMAL MAGIC · The victim must ask each person in the room what their favourite animal is and do an impression of each.

―――――――― SOME EQUINE NOMENCLATURE ――――――――

Colt ...... male, aged 4 and under, not castrated, not mated with a mare
Dam .... a horse's mother
Filly.. female up to the age of 4
Gelding .... castrated male
Juvenile.................. 2-year-old [flat racing]; 3- or 4-year-old [jumps]
Maiden.. a horse yet to win a race
Mare.................. female 4 or older *or* any female that has been bred
Sire .... a horse's father
Stallion.. male that mates with mares

——— SOME MARBLES OF NOTE ———

Aggies.. *marbles fabricated from agate*
Alleys...................................... *marbles fabricated from alabaster*
Bumboozers.. *extra large marbles*
Cat's eyes...................... *clear marbles with a twist of colour inside*
Chinas................................... *marbles fabricated from china*
Clearies.............................. *clear glass marbles of a single colour*
Commies .... *common marbles, fabricated from clay*
Milkies.................................... *opaque, milky-white marbles*
Onion skins................... *coloured marbles, decorated with swirls*
Peewees .... *small marbles*
Sulfides .... *valuable marbles of clear glass with clay figures inside*

Marbles can also be employed as a remedy for snoring. Simply sew a marble into the collar of the snorer's nightshirt, and they will be discouraged from sleeping on their backs.

——— BUMPER-STICKER INNUENDO ———

A selection of bumper-sticker slogans advocated by sporting enthusiasts:

· ANGLERS do it in their wellies · ARCHERS do it with a quiver · BOXING PROMOTERS do it for the money · BRIDGE PLAYERS do it with a rubber · CARD SHARPS do it with sleight of hand · CHESS players do it all for the King · CLIMBERS do it up against the wall · CRESTA riders do it head first, face-down · CROQUET PLAYERS do it before they peg out · DARTS players do it on the oche · DECATHLETES do it over two days · DIVERS do it under pressure · DRAUGHTS PLAYERS do it with a huff · FENCERS do it with protection · FISHERMEN do it with their flies down · GAMBLERS do it until they go bust · GLIDERS keep it up all day · GOLFERS do it with an interlocking grip · HOCKEY PLAYERS do it with an Indian dribble · JOCKEYS do it with a whip · JUGGLERS do it with balls · KNIFE THROWERS do it with glamorous assistants · MOUNTAINEERS do it with crampons · PING-PONG PLAYERS do it with spin · POKER PLAYERS do it with a straight face · POT-HOLERS do it in the dark · RACING DRIVERS do it in pole position · RALLY NAVIGATORS do it with tulips · REFEREES do it with a whistle · RUGBY players do it with odd-shaped balls · SCRABBLE PLAYERS do it up and down · SKIERS do it on the piste · SNOOKER players need a long rest · SNORKELERS do it without coming up for air · SPIN BOWLERS do it with a Chinaman · SWIMMERS go to great lengths to do it · TENNIS players do it from love · TRAMPOLINISTS do it in the air · WALKERS do it with their feet on the ground · WATER SKIERS do it on the pull · WEIGHTLIFTERS do it with a clean snatch · WINDSURFERS do it standing up · YACHTSWOMEN do it with buoys ·

CHOOSING 'it'

Many playground games, not least 'it' (see p.144), use elaborate procedures to select the 'infected' child. Apart from rock, paper, scissors (see p.128), a range of rhymes or 'dips' are employed to determine the odd one out:

Eeny meeny macker racker
Rare rie domi nacker
Chicker bocker lolli popper
Om pom push

Horcum, borcum,
curious corkum,
Herricum, berricum, buzz;
Eggs, butter, cheese, bread,
Stick, stock, stone dead.
[AMERICAN]

Red, white and blue
The cat's got the flu
The dog's got chicken pox,
So out goes YOU!

El, el, eopéné,
Sovouk sooya sagsama,
Gidém Haléb yolena;
Haléb dedi guin Pazar.
Haidé boona check boune
[ARMENIAN]

One potato, two potato,
Three potato, four
Five potato, six potato
Seven potato, more!

Your shoes are dirty,
Your shoes are clean,
Your shoes are not fit
To be seen by the Queen.

'Ekkero, akai-ri, you, kair-an
Filiussin, follasy, Nicholas ja'n
Kivi, kavi, Irishman,
Stini, Stani, buck.
[ROMANY]

Ickery, ahry, oary, ah,
Biddy, barber, oary, sah,
Peer, peer, mizter, meer,
Pit, pat, out, one.

Ichiku, tachikio, tayemosaro,
otoshime, samaga, chiugara,
mo, ni, owarite, kikeba,
hoho, hara, no, kai.
[JAPANESE]

CROQUET IN AMERICA

During the 1860s croquet swept across the Atlantic into America, where it was immediately embraced by most as a truly elegant and fashionable sport and, above all, a great civiliser. The New York periodical *Galaxy* declared in 1867 that 'croquet is an essentially social game, provocative of good humour, wit and fellowship, one in which old men forget their gout, young ones their bills unpaid; in which old ladies trip gayly across the sod in the chase of an 'enemy' ... in which the young ones blend duty and enjoyment so evenly that health blooms in their cheeks, lustre in their eyes, and renewed life throbs in every elastic step'. One manual of croquet went even further, claiming that croquet was 'a protection from evil influences by keeping all members in the household ranks ... [since] with rational amusements at home, no-one will be inclined to seek irrational ones abroad'. Not all, however, were so enamoured. In 1878, the *American Christian Review* enumerated the inevitable disastrous consequences of social activities such as croquet in the following manner:

a social party
social & party play
croquet party
picnic & croquet party
picnic, croquet, & dance
absence from church
imprudent or immoral conduct
exclusion from the church
a runaway match
poverty & discontent
shame & disgrace
ruin

In 1867, the Commissioners of New York's Central Park made a generous exception to their normal prohibition of active adult sports, by allowing girls to play croquet in secluded areas – away from main thoroughfares – on Wednesday and Friday afternoons.

— ATHLONS —

Biathlon	skiing, shooting
Triathlon (standard)	swimming 3-8km, cycling 180km, marathon run 42.195 km
Tetrathlon	riding, shooting, swimming, running
Pentathlon (traditional)	jump, javelin throw, 200-metre race, discus throw, 1,500-metre flat race
Pentathlon (modern)	showjumping, fencing, pistol shooting, 200m swim, 3,000m cross-country run
Pentathlon (women)	shot put, high jump, 100m hurdles, 800m race, long jump
Pentathlon (ancient)	running (c.200yds), long jump, discus, javelin, wrestling
Heptathlon (women)	[day 1] 100m hurdles, shot put, high jump, 200m race; [day2] long jump, javelin, 800m race
Decathlon	[day 1] 100m, long jump, shot put, high jump, 400m; [day 2] 110m hurdles, discus, pole vault, javelin, 1,500m

— TOP TRUMP PACKS —

Top Trumps have been a mainstay of school playgrounds since 1977. Below some classic and modern packs are deconstructed:

Pack name	Top Trump Categories · example cards
HORROR	Physical Strength · Fear Factor · Killing Power · Horror Rating · *Dracula · Lord of Death · The Freak*
PREHISTORIC MONSTERS	Existed · Length · Weight · Food · *Megaceros · Palaeoloxodon Euparkeria · Dipterus*
FROGS & TOADS	Length · Weight · Lifespan · Slime-o-Meter · *Tomato Frog · Dead Leaf Toad · Harlequin Frog*
SUPERHEROES	Strength · Powers · Weapons · *The Abomination · The Red Skull · Doctor Strange · Doctor Octopus*
SIMPSONS	Most Loveable · Smartest · Fattest · Biggest Nerd · Greatest Anarchist · Walk of Fame Rating · *Ned Flanders*
ROALD DAHL GOODIES & BADDIES	Brains · Kindness · Appearance · Greed · Cunning · RD Rating · *Roly-Poly Bird*
THE BEANO	Menacing · Softness · Dodging · Grub Scoffing · Brains · Beano star rating · *Rasher · Cuthbert Cringeworthy*

THE SPORT OF KINGS & OTHER NICKNAMES

The Sport of Kings[1] .... horse racing
The Noble Art[2] .... boxing
The Gentle Craft[3] .... angling
The Beautiful Game[4] .... football
The Noble Science of Defence .... fencing
The Tesserarian Art[5] .... gambling

[1] The Sport of Kings has been the nickname for a number of activities – some more sporting than others. In the C17th the term was a euphemism for WAR. Later, perhaps through belligerent associations with cavalry horses, the term was applied to HUNTING, although FALCONRY also enjoyed similar royal associations. Nowadays HORSE RACING and occasionally POLO are the sports most commonly linked with the phrase. Curiously, SURFING was dubbed the Sport of Kings as early as 1935, at least according to an article of that year in the magazine *Hawaiian Surfboard*. It seems that this unlikely association arose because surfing was traditionally the exclusive recreation of the Hawaiian royal family. TEN-PIN BOWLING's claim to the Sport of Kings probably rests on the first (or middle) pin, which is known as the kingpin (see p.130). Riders of the CRESTA RUN (see p.55) consider their pursuit the King of Winter Sports. [2] In addition to BOXING, the Noble Art has also been associated with SELF-DEFENCE, KITE FLYING, BILBOQUET (cup-and-ball), and THIMBLERIGGERY (sleight-of-hand contricks). [3] It has been suggested that this nickname might be a pun on the word 'gentle' – a term for the maggots (the larvae of the flesh-fly or bluebottle) which were traditionally employed by anglers as bait. Izaak Walton (1593–1683), author of *The Compleat Angler*, a classic pastoral account of fishing, was bestowed the monicker 'The Gentle'. Angling should of course not be confused with the Gentle Art of Persuasion or, indeed, the *Gentle Art of Making Enemies*, 1890, by James McNeill Whistler. [4] Dutch footballer Ruud Gullit extended the notion of the Beautiful Game by coining the phrase 'sexy football' to describe his vision of the game. This is not to be confused with the other Dutch notion of 'total football' popularised in the 1970s, that advocated an all-rounder approach to player skills and positions. PELOTA (or JAI ALAI) has on occasion been called the Beautiful Game. [5] An archaic term which derives from the Latin for dice *tesserae* (see p.116).

HANDKERCHIEFS AND BULLFIGHTS

In the language of bullfighting the *pañuelo* is a handkerchief used by the *presidente* (adjudicator) of the fight to signal his orders. A WHITE *pañuelo* is used to signal the start of the parade; the release of the bulls; and the various stages of the fight. And, once the bull is dead, one wave of the WHITE *pañuelo* signals the *matador* will be awarded one ear; two waves signals both ears; three waves signals both ears and the tail. A GREEN *pañuelo* signals that the bull is to be returned to the corrals because it is defective or because it cannot be killed. A RED *pañuelo* signals that larger *banderillas* (spiked sticks) must be used to coax a recalcitrant bull to charge – an act which brings disgrace both to the bull and its breeder.

—— COMPARATIVE BALL SIZE SCHEMATIC ——

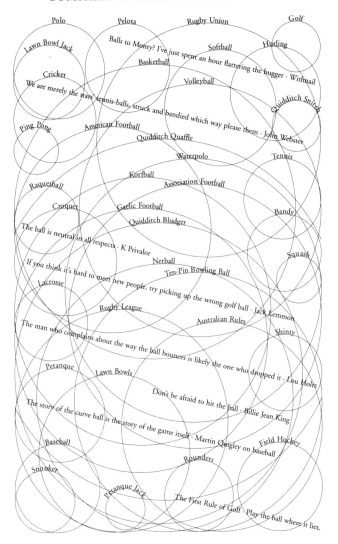

The schematic is based on the maximum circumference of the ball. Scale: 1mm ≈ 10mm

GLADIATORS

Unique to Roman culture, gladiators originated at funerals (in *c.*264BC) when combat displays replaced sacrifices. The popularity of the grim and bloody gladiatorial games became such a part of Roman life that in AD326 Constantine felt the need to suppress them. The gladiators themselves were criminals, slaves, or prisoners of war, and most did not survive for very long. Occasionally, victorious fighters developed a certain fame, earning money, gifts, and visits from women. However, their ultimate goal was to receive the *rudis* – a wooden sword which conferred freedom. A variety of gladiators fought against each other (as well as wild animals):

Andabata · 'Blind-fighters' who wore full helmets with no eye-holes; their challenge was to fight using their remaining senses.

Eques · Fought on horseback with a 2-metre-long lance and sword. They wore helmets and had fabric wrappings on their lower legs.

Samnite · Took their name from a tribe defeated by the Romans in 312BC. They wore plumed helmets, carried large oblong shields and fought with a sword.

Myrmillo · 'Fish man', so called due to a distinctive fin-like crest on their helmets. They were equipped with a large shield and fought with a sword.

Thracian · Fought with a short curved sword and wore a wide-brimmed helmet with crest.

Secutor · 'Chasers', they carried a dagger and wore only a helmet, metal guards on the left leg and padding on the sword arm.

Retiarius · Lightly armed and mobile, they wore no helmet and only their sword arm and shoulder were protected. They were armed with a net and trident.

Provocator · Known as 'challengers' they wore helmets with visors and breast-plates, and carried round shields and straight-edged swords.

Hoplomachus · Heavily armoured with metal guards on their lower legs and fabric wrapping on their thighs and sword arm. They fought with a lance and dagger.

Bestiarii · The lowest-ranking gladiators, they fought wild beasts with only whips or spears.

Debate rages over the role of the thumb in gladiatorial arenas since no conclusive pictorial evidence has been unearthed. It seems that when a gladiator fell he would appeal to the mercy of the crowd with a raised index finger. Most sources agree that, in response, the crowd would either 'press the thumb' or 'turn the thumb', but it is unclear what these meant. It is often claimed that an upturned thumb meant death and a downturned thumb life – though the opposite explanation is to be found in many sources. In Ridley Scott's *Gladiator* (2000) an upturned thumb signified life and vice versa. Here, the life of Gladiator Maximus (Russell Crowe) is spared when the crowd chant 'save' and make a thumbs-up gesture, thus compelling Emperor Commodus to spare the life of his enemy.

─────────── 'ETON BOATING SONG' ───────────

The *Eton Boating Song* was written in 1863 by William Johnson Cory with music by Captain Algernon Drummond. The song is occasionally sung at Eton College dinners and concerts, and is sometimes played at the Procession of Boats – traditionally held on the 4th June, the birthday of George III. Here, crews row past Fellows' Eyot, where they stand upright in their boats, shaking fresh flowers from their boaters into the water.

Jolly boating weather
And a hay harvest breeze
Blade on the feather
Shade off the trees
Swing swing together
With your backs between your knees
Swing swing together
With your backs between your knees

Rugby may be more clever
Harrow may make more row
But we'll row for ever
Steady from stroke to bow
And nothing in life shall sever
The chain that is round us now
And nothing in life shall sever
The chain that is round us now

Others will fill our places
Dress'd in the old light blue
We'll recollect our races
We'll to the flag be true
And youth will be still in our faces
When we cheer for an Eton crew
And youth will be still in our faces
When we cheer for an Eton crew

Twenty years hence this weather
May tempt us from our stools
We may be slow on the feather
And seem to the boys old fools
But we'll still swing together
And swear by the best of schools
But we'll still swing together
And swear by the best of schools

[Verses 1, 6, 7, & 8 are those usually sung.] Henry 'Blowers' Blofeld selected the song as one of his Desert Island Discs. His book was *A Pelican at Blandings* by P.G. Wodehouse.

─────────── NAISMITH'S RULE ───────────

W.W. Naismith, a founder of the Scottish Mountaineering Club, devised a formula to enable walkers in hilly or mountainous regions to estimate the time required for an expedition. The premise of Naismith's Rule was to allow one hour for every 5km (3 miles) measured on the map plus an additional half-hour for every 300m (1,000ft) ascended. For example:

10km ($\therefore$2h) on map + 870m ($\therefore$1½h) climb = 3½ hours

Naturally this formula assumes reasonable fitness, good weather, a group of equal speed, good conditions underfoot, and a bearable weight of pack. Most consider Naismith to have been either remarkably bullish or just plain optimistic, and many expeditions cautiously add 50% extra time. A host of other walkers (Aitken, Tranter, Langmuir, Kennedy, et al.) have proposed more sophisticated methods of calculation that take into account such factors as type of terrain underfoot, speed of descent, seasonal variations, headwind, fatigue, weather conditions, and so on.

—————————— EQUESTRIAN CRICKET ——————————

A very singular game of cricket will be played on Tuesday, the 6th May, in Linsted Park, between the Gentlemen of the Hill and the Gentlemen of the Dale, for one guinea a man. The whole will be played on horseback. To begin at nine o'clock, and the game to be played out. A good ordinary on the ground by John Hobgen.

— Advertisement, *The Kentish Gazette,* 29 April 1794

—————————— 'it' ——————————

There are any number of versions of the playground game 'it', all of which are based on the premise that one player is 'it' – and 'it' is very contagious.

SAFETY · where players are safe if they are touching an agreed object. However, only one person can touch the object at any time.

JOIN ME · where any player who is touched by 'it' becomes 'it' *as well.* The last uninfected player wins.

CONGA · players who are touched by 'it' must clasp 'it' around the waist and join them in their pursuit. In this way, an 'it' conga-line forms; but only the first and last in the line can 'it' another.

BALL · best played in an enclosed space, 'it' is armed with a tennis or football, and 'it' is transferred to the first player that the ball touches. Clearly, 'it' must carefully judge the violence of their throws.

STATUES · an agreed number of the pursued are deemed statues, who are immune from 'it' but must remain motionless. Others can seek respite from the chase by tapping a statue on the shoulder and swapping places, at which time the former statue is fair game.

STICK IN MUD · a player who is touched by 'it' becomes stuck in a star-jump position, and can only be unstuck from the mud by another player crawling through their legs. If 'it' manages to stick all the players in the mud, the last player to be stuck becomes 'it'.

OFF THE GROUND · Players are safe from 'it' if both of their feet are off the ground; manhole covers count, but jumping does not.

—————————— THE 1569 LOTTERY ——————————

The first English lottery consisted of 400,000 lots priced at 10 shillings. It was drawn in 1569 at the West Door of St Paul's. The prizes were given in plate, and the proceeds went to repairing ports around the kingdom.

—DRAG RACE CATEGORIES & CHRISTMAS TREES—

Drag racing is a straight-line contest of raw acceleration between two vehicles over a measured distance – usually ¼ mile (1,320'), or ⅛ mile (660'). A vast array of classes and categories exist (which differ between race organisers), but there are four basic classes of professional drag cars:

TOP FUEL · the ultimate cars for drag racing, they can travel from a standing start to 100mph in under a second. They are fueled by nitro-methane, of which they can burn 15 gallons (*c.*$500) each race.

FUNNY CAR · supercharged cars fuelled by methanol or ethanol and clad in fibreglass or carbon fibre. They can travel ¼ mile in 5·7 seconds at over 240mph.

PRO STOCK · two-door coupé or sedan street cars, less than 5 years old, with gas-burning carburettor engines that can generate over 200mph. Because of its link with production cars, pro-stock class is considered a purist's category.

PRO MODIFIED · a diverse class of vehicles with modified engines and chassis, some with supercharging or nitrous oxide injection.

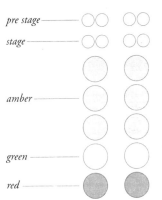

pre stage
stage
amber
green
red

Races are started and timed by lights called the 'Christmas tree'. When an infrared beam about 9" from the start-line is broken the *pre-stage* lights are lit. A second beam on the start-line triggers the *stage* lights when the front of the tyre breaks it. (When the front tyre crosses this beam, the car's time starts.) The three *amber* lights illuminate together to indicate that the race is about to begin, and 0·4 seconds later the *green* go light is lit. If cars cross the line before *green,* the *red* foul light comes on.

——————— HOURS REQUIRED FOR SLEEP ———————

A *traveller* five hours doth crave,
To sleep, a *student* seven will have,
And nine sleeps every idle *knave.*

or

Nature requires six · *Custom* seven · *Laziness* nine · and *Wickedness* eleven

———————— ARROBAS ————————

Arrobas are the units used to weigh fighting bulls in Spain. 1 *arroba* is roughly equal to 25lbs; the ideal weight for a bull is said to be 30 *arrobas*.

———— BBC SPORTS PERSONALITY OF THE YEAR ————

1954	Chris Chataway	1979	Sebastian Coe
1955	Gordon Pirie	1980	Robin Cousins
1956	Jim Laker	1981	Ian Botham
1957	Dai Rees	1982	Daley Thompson
1958	Ian Black	1983	Steve Cram
1959	John Surtees	1984	Torvill & Dean
1960	David Broome	1985	Barry McGuigan
1961	Stirling Moss	1986	Nigel Mansell
1962	Anita Lonsbrough	1987	Fatima Whitbread
1963	Dorothy Hyman	1988	Steve Davis
1964	Mary Rand	1989	Nick Faldo
1965	Tommy Simpson	1990	Paul Gascoigne
1966	Bobby Moore	1991	Liz McColgan
1967	Henry Cooper	1992	Nigel Mansell
1968	David Hemery	1993	Linford Christie
1969	Ann Jones	1994	Damon Hill
1970	Henry Cooper	1995	Jonathan Edwards
1971	Princess Anne†	1996	Damon Hill
1972	Mary Peters	1997	Greg Rusedski
1973	Jackie Stewart	1998	Michael Owen
1974	Brendan Foster	1999	Lennox Lewis
1975	David Steele	2000	Steve Redgrave
1976	John Curry	2001	David Beckham
1977	Virginia Wade	2002	Paula Radcliffe
1978	Steve Ovett	2003	Jonny Wilkinson

† Princess Anne participated in the 1976 Olympics, and is one of few recent Olympians of whom a genetic sex-test was not required. On being a royal sportswoman she has said: 'It is difficult to control the horse at the best of times – and the horse is about the only person who does not know you are royal.' And, 'When I appear in public people expect me to neigh, grind my teeth, paw the ground and swish my tail – none of which is easy.'

———— OLYMPIC SWIMMING POOL SPECIFICATIONS ————

Length	50m	Lane width	2.5m
Width	25m	Water temperature	25°–28°C
Number of lanes	8	Light intensity	>1500 lux

—————— BELOW THE BELT ——————

The boxing belt is an imaginary line from the navel to the top of the hips.

—————— TANGRAM PUZZLES ——————

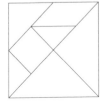

The Tangram or Anchor Enigma is a traditional Chinese puzzle that consists of a square dissected into seven shapes: five triangles, a square, and a rhombus. (The Chinese name *Ch'i ch'iao t'u* translates as 'seven ingenious plan'.) Several hundred shapes can be made from these pieces (all of which have to be used), but some of the most complex are those that seem the simplest:

[For the solution to these classic tangram puzzles, turn to p.160.]

—————— SPORTING NELSONS ——————

The term Nelson appears in a number of sports most notably, of course, in cricket and wrestling. Viscount Horatio Nelson (1758–1805) was the Admiral who commanded the English navy throughout the French Revolutionary War and in the early stages of the Napoleonic War; he died at the Battle of Trafalgar, where the English routed the combined fleets of France and Spain. Nelson lost sight in his right eye at the Battle of Calvi (1794), and his right arm trying to take Santa Cruz (1797) – wounds that defined the indomitable spirit of the English seaman and, somehow, crossed into the world of sport. In cricket, a Nelson is the score of 111 (also 222 and 333), and it probably derives from Nelson's monocular and monobrachial state. When batsmen reach this score some superstitiously lift their feet off the ground; the umpire David Shepherd even performs a little dance. (For Australian batsmen 87 is an unlucky number, possibly because it is 13 short of a century). The world of wrestling is replete with Nelsons – quarter-Nelson, half-Nelson, three-quarter-Nelson, and full-Nelson – which are holds in which wrestlers interlock their arms around the neck of their opponents. (The schoolboy's idea of a Nelson is where one or two arms are twisted at right angles behind the back.) For a period, 'one-armed bandit' gambling machines were also nicknamed Nelsons.

——— ON DREAMS AND DREAMING———

CARL JUNG · Your vision will become clear only when you can look into your own heart ... Who looks outside, dreams; who looks inside, awakes.

RALPH WALDO EMERSON · Judge of your natural character by what you do in your dreams.

JOAN DIDION · We all have the same dreams.

WILLIAM DEMENT · Dreaming permits each and every one of us to be quietly and safely insane every night of our lives.

SADIE DELANY · In our dreams, we are always young.

W.B. YEATS · I have spread my dreams under your feet. Tread softly because you tread on my dreams.

HENRY DAVID THOREAU · If one advances confidently in the direction of his dreams, and endeavours to live the life which he has imagined, he will meet with a success unexpected in common hours.

HENRIK IBSEN · Castles in the air – they're so easy to take refuge in. So easy to build, too.

WILLIAM SHAKESPEARE · We are such stuff As dreams are made on; and our little life Is rounded with a sleep.
[*The Tempest*, IV.i.]

STEPHEN VINCENT BENÉT · Dreaming men are haunted men.

BOB DYLAN · I am against nature. I don't dig nature at all. I think nature is very unnatural. I think the truly natural things are dreams, which nature can't touch with decay.

CHUANG TSE · I do not know whether I was then a man dreaming I was a butterfly, or whether I am now a butterfly dreaming I am a man.

FRIEDRICH NIETZSCHE · I fly in dreams, I know it is my privilege, I do not recall a single situation in dreams when I was unable to fly. To execute every sort of curve and angle with a light impulse, a flying mathematics – that is so distinct a happiness that it has permanently suffused my basic sense of happiness.

GEORGE BERNARD SHAW · You see things; and you say Why? But I dream things that never were; and I say Why not?

JOHN UPDIKE · Dreams come true; without that possibility, nature would not incite us to have them.

GÉRARD DE NERVAL · Dreams are a second life. I have never been able to penetrate without a shudder those ivory or horned gates which separate us from the invisible world.

ON DREAMS AND DREAMING cont.

MARCEL PROUST · If a little dreaming is dangerous, the cure for it is not to dream less but to dream more, to dream all the time.

VICTOR HUGO · To substitute day-dreaming for thought is to confuse a poison with a source of nourishment.

STEPHEN BROOK · Unpinned even by rudimentary notions of time and space, dreams float or flash by, leaving in their wake trails of unease, hopes, fears and anxieties.

T.E. LAWRENCE · All men dream: but not equally. Those who dream by night in the dusty recesses of their minds wake in the day to find that it was vanity: but the dreamers of the day are dangerous men, for they may act their dream with open eyes, to make it possible.

ERICH FROMM · Both dreams and myths are important communications from ourselves to ourselves. If we do not understand the language in which they are written, we miss a great deal of what we know and tell ourselves in those hours when we are not busy manipulating the outside world.

MICHEL DE MONTAIGNE · I hold that it is true that dreams are faithful interpreters of our drives; but there is an art to sorting and understanding them.

VIRGINIA WOOLF · Yet it is in our idleness, in our dreams, that the submerged truth sometimes comes to the top.

SIGMUND FREUD · Interpretation of dreams is the royal road to a knowledge of the unconscious activities of the mind. (See p.77.)

SOME HORSE-RACING COLOURS

Sheikh Mohammed ...... maroon, white sleeves; maroon cap, white star
The Macca & Growler Ptnshp[†] .... white; white cap, royal blue star
Vinnie Jones (The Shooting Party) .... light blue, red disc; red cap
Lord and Lady Lloyd-Webber............................ pink, grey sash
Prince of Wales .... scarlet, royal blue sleeves; black cap
Robert Sangster .... green, blue sleeves; white cap, green spots
Sir Clement Freud ... black, orange hoop sleeves; black cap, orange spots
J.P. McManus .... emerald green, orange hoops; white cap
Ronnie Wood .... white, red sash, white sleeves, red seams
Khaled Abdullah .... green, pink sash,white sleeves; pink cap
HM The Queen .... purple & gold, scarlet sleeves; black & gold cap
HH Aga Khan .... green, red epaulettes
Sir Peter O'Sullevan .... black, yellow cross belts; yellow cap

† The nickname of the partnership of footballers Steve McManaman and Robbie Fowler.

--------- A FATHER'S ADVICE TO HIS SON ---------

Mark Hanbury Beaufoy (1854–1922), MP for Kennington (1889–95), wrote these lines for his eldest son, Henry Mark Beaufoy, on giving him a gun:

If a sportsman true you'd be, Listen carefully to me:

Never, never let your gun
Pointed be at anyone;
That it may unloaded be
Matters not the least to me.

When a hedge or fence you cross,
Though of time it cause a loss,
From your gun the cartridge take,
For the greater safety's sake.

If twixt you and neighbouring gun,
Birds may fly or beasts may run
Let this maxim e'er be thine:
Follow not across the line.

Stops and beaters oft unseen
Lurk behind some leafy screen;
Calm and steady always be:
Never shoot where you can't see.

Keep your place and silent be:
Game can hear and game can see;
Don't be greedy, better spared
Is a pheasant than one shared.

You may kill or you may miss,
But at all times think of this:
All the pheasants ever bred
Won't repay for one man dead.

--------------- NIM ---------------

Although the game probably originated in China – where it is known as *Tsyanshidzi* – Nim was named and popularised in 1901 by the mathematician C.L. Bouton, who used it to explore binary. Nim is a deceptively simple game for two that can be played with any set of similar objects from cards or matches to pebbles or coins. (The game's name derives from the German *nehmen* – to take.) The objects are laid as opposite, and the players take turns in removing any number of objects they like *from one row only.* The player who removes the last object is the loser (or winner, depending on which version is played). The most stylish game of Nim is that played in Alain Resnais' 1962 film classic *L'année dernière à Marienbad,* which has the following dialogue: 'I know a game I always win.' – 'If you can't lose, it's no game.' – 'I can lose, but I always win.'

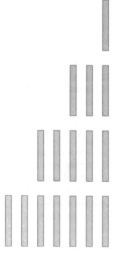

―――――――――― CORINTHIANS ――――――――――

In addition to delineating an ornate order of Greek columns, the term Corinthian is used in the world of sport to describe a keen, often wealthy, usually fashionable, amateur. From at least the C16th, Corinthian had a definite pejorative tone and it was employed to damn a class of idle and utterly shameless fornicators. Francis Grose, in his 1785 *Dictionary of the Vulgar Tongue*, describes Corinthians as 'frequenters of brothels; also an impudent brazen faced fellow'. It seems these associations derived from the louche behaviour popularly held to be endemic in Greek and Roman Corinth. Over time, the term became less harsh and it was used to describe both fashionable 'swells' and dilettante sportsmen. Nowadays, a number of amateur sports teams dub themselves Corinthians, though in the United States, Corinthianism tends to be associated with yachting.

―――――――――― SOME CHESS QUOTATIONS ――――――――――

NIGEL SHORT · Chess is ruthless: you've got to be prepared to kill people.

SHERLOCK HOLMES · Excellence at chess is one mark of a scheming mind.

JAMIE MURPHY · Chess, like mathematics and music, is a nursery for child prodigies.

INDIAN PROVERB · Chess is a sea in which a gnat may drink and an elephant may bathe.

BOBBY FISCHER · I like the moment when I break a man's ego.

GEORGE BERNARD SHAW · [chess] is a foolish expedient for making idle people believe they are doing something clever when they are only wasting their time.

LENIN · Chess is the gymnasium of the mind.

THOMAS FULLER · When a man's house is on fire, it's time to break off the chess.

―――――――――― JANE AUSTEN ON BASEBALL vs BOOKS ――――――――――

... it was not very wonderful that Catherine, who had by nature nothing heroic about her, should prefer cricket, baseball, riding on horseback, and running about the country at the age of fourteen, to books – or at least books of information – for, provided that nothing like useful knowledge could be gained from them, provided they were all story and no reflection, she had never any objection to books at all.

— JANE AUSTEN, *Northanger Abbey*, 1818

—— A HIERARCHY OF ACTION AND INACTION ——

A host of Victorian writers were preoccupied with the dangers both of an idleness and overactivity. Below is one of many guides to a 'decent' life:

† DEATH †	VIGOUR	PASSIVITY
CONVULSION	EAGERNESS	INDIFFERENCE
MANIA	VIM	ATARAXIA
FRENZY	ENTHUSIASM	FALLOWNESS
APOPLEXY	INDUSTRIOUSNESS	APATHY
MALESTROM	ACTIVITY	SHIFTLESSNESS
TUMULT	LABOUR	AIMLESSNESS
TURMOIL	EMPLOYMENT	DORMANCY
ANXIETY	DUTY	FIXITY
HYPERACTIVITY	PRAYER	DESULTORINESS
UPSET		LAZINESS
DISCOMPOSURE		IDLENESS
PERTURBATION	· THE BALANCED LIFE OF A HUMBLE AND DEVOTED PENITENT ·	INDOLENCE
AGITATION	G	INERTIA
EXCITATION	GOD	SLUGGARDNESS
NERVOUSNESS	D	CUNCTATIVE
DISCOMFITURE		INATTENTION
UNQUIETNESS	PRAYER	TORPOR
BUSTLE	SERENITY	AESTIVATION
HUSTLE	TRANQUILLITY	NUMBNESS
FIDGETINESS	EQUIPOISE	STAGNANCY
CLUTTER	PLACIDITY	OSSIFICATION
CROWDEDNESS	CONTEMPLATION	VEGETATION
BOTHERATION	QUIETISM	INSENSIBILITY
AMBITION	QUIESCENCE	UNCONSCIOUSNESS
ANIMATION	PHLEGMATICISM	COMA
VIVACITY	IMPERTURBABILITY	† DEATH †

MORNINGTON CRESCENT

If you've understood Mornington Crescent,
nothing else in your life makes sense.
— JEREMY HARDY

Few pastimes combine sporting, gaming, and idling as perfectly as the game of *Mornington Crescent*. Since the early days of its play, the game has proved a test of mental agility, geographical and topological awareness, strategic thinking, and psychological manoeuvring. Paul Merton once described *Mornington Crescent* as 'chess for the mind', and analysts have drawn comparisons with Sun Tzu's teachings in *The Art of War*, and the work of Phyllis Pearsall, who first mapped the *London A–Z*. The game's popular appeal is largely due to its inclusion in the BBC Radio 4 show *I'm Sorry I Haven't a Clue*. Here the undisputed grand-masters are Graeme Garden, Barry Cryer, Tim Brooke-Taylor, and the late Willie Rushton. Celebrated trumpeter Humph-'rey' Lyttleton is regarded as the foremost adjudicator on the somewhat Byzantine regulations of *Mornington Crescent* – not least 'Lord Grosvenor's Original Metropolitan Rules' and 'Hooper's Mainline Variation'. (However, Humph's passion for the game has been questioned as recent adjudications appear more uninterested than disinterested.) The game's deceptively simple premise (the first player to nominate Mornington Crescent wins) hides a multitude of tricks, traps, and subtle conventions. Below, Graeme Garden provides a few hints and tips for aspiring and regular players of *Mornington Crescent*:

SAFE PLAY – The 'percentage' player will be wise not to open laterals and diagonals in the same move. Baker Street is always a risky call in the late middle game, but can be a clincher during extended Crabbitt's progressions.

HIGH-RISK PLAY – 'Blind-looping' should only be attempted by an experienced partner, namely one who has mastered Fairlop's Last Theorem. 'Feathering the Metropolitan' can be exhilarating, but remember to keep an eye on your opponent's suburban linkage. Nobody wants to be caught 'Stovolding' in Nip! If in doubt, invoke the Chatham House Rule.

DEEP PLAY – This is the basis of the game as practised at Club and County level. Time limits are applied to all moves apart from conjunctions, and the game may therefore be won or lost on compound penalties. It is thus prudent to forgo all attempts to meld terminals, and straddling the circle should never be contemplated without Parson's Green being held.

EXTREME PLAY – Is to be discouraged.

Stovold's Mornington Crescent Almanac, edited by Graeme Garden, 1991, is accepted as the ultimate authority on *Mornington Crescent* game-play strategy.

'Make a long arm, Watson, and see what V has to say.' I leaned back and took down the great index volume to which he referred. Holmes balanced it on his knee, and his eyes moved slowly and lovingly over the record of old cases, mixed with the accumulated information of a lifetime. 'Voyage of the *Gloria Scott*,' he read. 'That was a bad business … Victor Lynch the forger. Venomous lizard or gila. Remarkable case, that! Vittoria, the circus belle. Vanderbilt and the Yeggman. Vipers. Vigor, the Hammersmith wonder. Hullo! Hullo! Good old index. You can't beat it. Listen to this, Watson. Vampirism in Hungary. And again, Vampires in Transylvania.'

— ARTHUR CONAN DOYLE, *The Adventure of the Sussex Vampire*, 1924

———— ABIDE WITH ME – BULLFIGHTING ————

What readers ask nowadays in a book is that it should improve, instruct, and elevate. This book wouldn't elevate a cow. I cannot conscientiously recommend it for any useful purposes whatever. All I can suggest is that when you get tired of reading 'the best hundred books' you may take this up for half an hour. It will be a change.

— JEROME K. JEROME, *Idle Thoughts of an Idle Fellow*, 1886

———— PROPORTION OF ENTRY TYPES ————

Sporting 46% · Gaming 28% · Idling 26%